insight text guide

Catriona Mills

The Yield

Tara June Winch

First published in 2022, reprinted in 2023.

Insight Publications Pty Ltd
3/350 Charman Road
Cheltenham VIC 3192
Australia
Tel: +61 3 8571 4950
Fax: +61 3 8571 0257
Email: books@insightpublications.com.au

www.insightpublications.com.au

A catalogue record for this book is available from the National Library of Australia

Tara June Winch's The Yield / Catriona Mills

Catriona Mills asserts the moral right to be identified as the author of this work.

ISBNs:
9781922771292 (print)
9781922771308 (digital)
9781922771315 (bundle: print + digital)

Cover design by Melisa Paredes

Printed by Markono Print Media Pte Ltd

contents

CHARACTER MAP

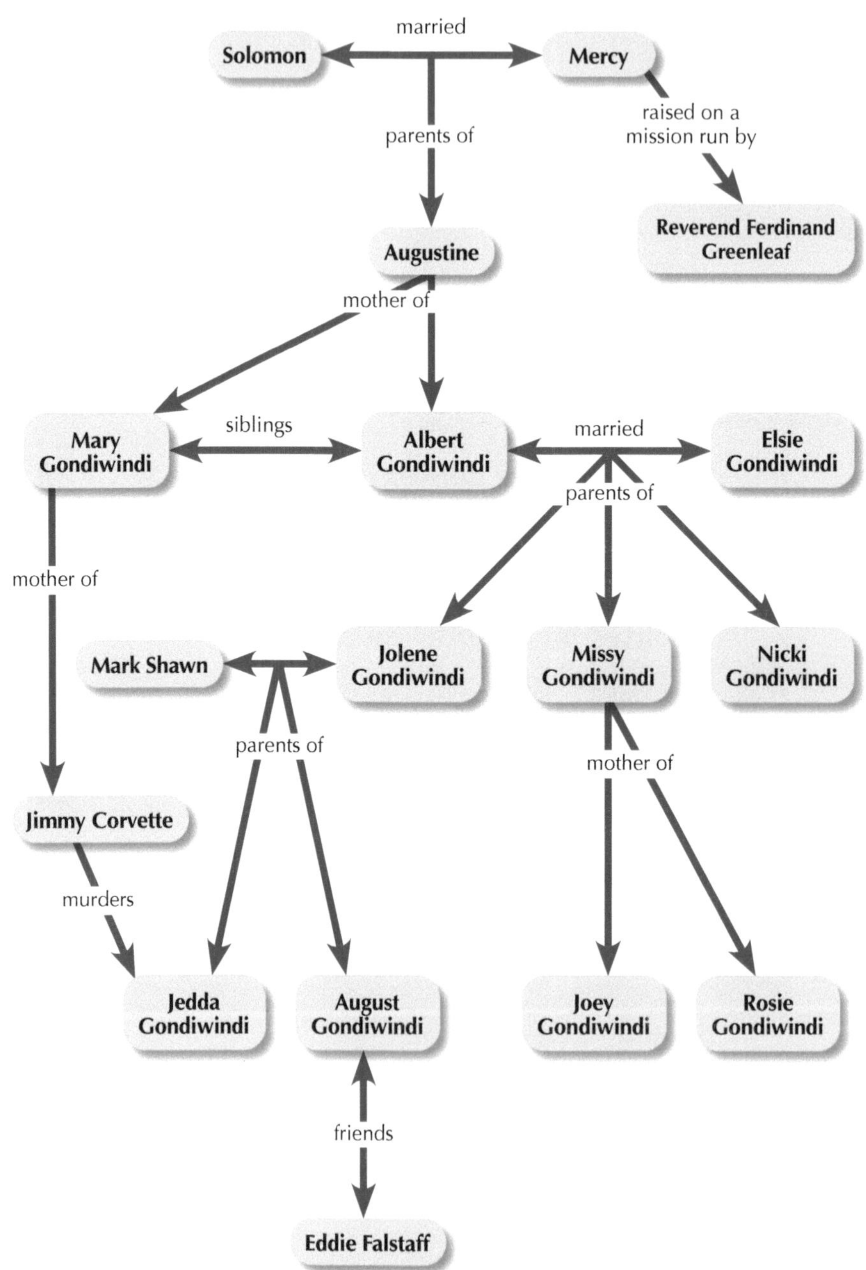

OVERVIEW

About the author

Wiradjuri writer Tara June Winch was born in Wollongong, and travelled across Australia in her late teens. She was studying for a Bachelor of Arts in Indigenous Studies at Gnibi College, Southern Cross University, when she won the David Unaipon Award in 2004 and stopped studying in order to pursue writing. She has published two short-story collections in addition to her debut novel, *The Yield* (2019). As well as writing, she has been an ambassador for the Indigenous Literacy Foundation and Children's Ground, both Indigenous-led organisations with a strong focus on community and on the welfare of children. Winch has been based in France for several years.

Winch's first work was *Swallow the Air* (University of Queensland Press, 2006), a series of interlinked short stories about a young Aboriginal girl who, after her mother's death, journeys across Australia and into inner Sydney, the Northern Territory and central New South Wales. As a manuscript, *Swallow the Air* won the prestigious David Unaipon Award (for an unpublished Indigenous author), and it later won a Victorian Premier's Literary Award, a NSW Premier's Literary Award and the 2007 Dobbie Literary Award, as well as collecting a series of short-listings. After publishing *Swallow the Air*, Winch undertook a mentorship with Nobel Prize–winning Nigerian author Wole Soyinka.

Another short-story collection, *After the Carnage* (University of Queensland Press, 2016), was highly commended at the Victorian Premier's Literary Awards and short-listed for both the Queensland Literary Awards and the NSW Premier's Literary Awards. But *The Yield* was more successful again, winning three NSW Premier's Literary Awards (including the Book of the Year and People's Choice Awards), the Voss Literary Prize, the Prime Minister's Literary Award for Fiction and the prestigious Miles Franklin Literary Award.

Synopsis

At the end of his life, after being diagnosed with terminal pancreatic cancer, Albert 'Poppy' Gondiwindi sits down to write a dictionary of the Wiradjuri language. August receives news of her grandfather's death and flies from England to the family home, Prosperous House, on Massacre Plains, where her grandmother Elsie is living alone. August has not been home for ten years. The property, the site of a former Lutheran mission, is about to be taken over by Rinepalm Mining, and Elsie must leave Prosperous House. As August prepares for her grandfather's funeral and helps Elsie pack up the home, she is haunted by memories of her sister, Jedda, who went missing when they were children and whose body has never been found. She finds herself having to face old family secrets that she had tried to escape by running away from home; she is also dealing with an ongoing eating disorder that predates Jedda's disappearance but has been exacerbated by it. She rekindles a fraught friendship with Eddie Falstaff, who lives at the neighbouring property, Southerly House, and she crosses the path of the protestors camped nearby, waiting to protest against the tin mine when the machinery moves in.

August becomes aware of the existence of her grandfather's dictionary, which has disappeared, and that he had hoped to stop the mine from proceeding by demonstrating the Gondiwindis' ongoing connection to Massacre Plains and lodging a Native Title claim. She reconnects with her nana as well as her great aunt (Albert's sister, Mary), her aunts Missy and Nicki, and her cousin Joey.

After a disastrous sexual encounter with her old friend Eddie Falstaff, August learns that the Falstaffs have been donating Gondiwindi artefacts to a Sydney museum for over a century. She and Aunt Missy travel to the museum but are given a series of forms to request access to the artefacts, leaving them anxious that there will not be enough time to use them to stop the mine, especially since the mine is supported by the other townspeople. When they return to Prosperous House, they find that the mining company has already begun clearing land, and that the protestors have set fire to the fields. They and Joey join the protestors, chaining themselves to the fence as the bulldozers move in. Nicki arrives with Albert's dictionary, which reveals not only the family's long-running ties to the land but also Jedda's fate. As the bulldozer knocks over the final tree, it exposes a long-lost and never-mapped cemetery dating back to the days of the Mission, which provides a basis for delaying the mine and making a land claim. August decides not to return to Europe but to remain with Elsie and her own mother, recently released from prison, and August and Joey distribute Albert's dictionary to the local children.

Interspersed with this narrative are sections of Albert's dictionary, which also recollect key moments in Albert's life; and a long letter from Reverend Greenleaf – the first missionary to run Prosperous House – written while he was incarcerated as a German 'enemy alien' during World War I.

Character summaries

Albert 'Poppy' Gondiwindi

The patriarch of the Gondiwindi family, Albert Gondiwindi dies from pancreatic cancer at the beginning of the novel, but acts as a narrator throughout, in the sections of his dictionary. Albert is the son of Augustine, who was the daughter of Mercy, one of the first children born at the Prosperous Mission. He is taken from Tent Town to the Mission as a child, and later separated from his mother and his younger sister, Mary. He is the husband of Elsie, father of Missy, Nicki and Jolene, uncle of Jimmy, and grandfather of Joey, Rosie, August and Jedda.

August Gondiwindi

The primary narrative focus for the part of the novel set in the present day, August Gondiwindi is the granddaughter of Albert and Elsie, with whom she lived from the age of eight, when her parents, Jolene and Mark, were arrested for growing marijuana. She is haunted by the disappearance of her sister Jedda when they were children, and becomes fascinated by her grandfather's missing manuscript.

Aunt Missy

Missy is the daughter of Albert and Elsie, and the mother of August's cousins Joey and Rosie. She is closely connected to her family at Prosperous House. A strong, outspoken woman, she opposes the mine and later joins the protest. She is angered by the news that Gondiwindi artefacts are locked away in the museum, and is proud of what her son achieves in his time in prison.

Aunt Nicki

The daughter of Albert and Elsie, Aunt Nicki is unmarried, elegant and self-possessed. She works at the local council offices. Nicki suppresses Albert's manuscript and the truth about what happened to Jedda, and later moves to the city.

Eddie Falstaff

Eddie is the son and heir of the Falstaffs, who own Southerly House, the big house up the hill from Prosperous Station. An old friend of August's, he has always been in love with her. He resents the fact that he is trapped in Massacre Plains by his connection to the house and land, and supports the presence of the mining company.

Elsie Gondiwindi

The wife of Albert, mother of Missy, Nicki and Jolene, and grandmother of Joey, Rosie, August and Jedda, Elsie Gondiwindi comes from Sydney, where she was involved in civil rights protests in the 1960s. She met Albert when she was part of the Freedom Ride. During the novel, she is grieving both for her husband and for the imminent loss of her home.

Reverend Ferdinand Greenleaf

A German-born Lutheran missionary, Greenleaf arrives in South Australia with his family as a child, and later sets up the mission at Prosperous. He is interned in a camp for 'enemy aliens' during World War I, where he writes a letter describing the history of the Mission.

Great Aunt Mary

The younger sister of Albert and mother of Jimmy, Aunt Mary has a close relationship with her sister-in-law Elsie. She adored Jimmy, but August feels that Aunt Mary 'didn't know about the bad in her own son' (p.60).

Jedda Gondiwindi

August had a close relationship with Jedda, her older sister. The girls went to live with Albert and Elsie when their parents were arrested for growing marijuana. Jedda disappeared as a girl, and the secret of her fate is known only to Albert, who reveals the story in his dictionary manuscript.

Joey Gondiwindi

The son of Aunt Missy, Joey spent four years in juvenile detention and jail for a crime that August and Eddie were also involved in (for which they were never caught). He studied in prison and has developed a computer game in which the user fights colonisers. He is estranged from his father but close to his grandfather, who visits him often in prison. Joey is infuriated by the mining company taking control of the land.

BACKGROUND & CONTEXT

Neither Aboriginal cultures nor Aboriginal people's experiences of colonial violence and trauma are monolithic. The Eora Nation (in the Sydney region) bore the first brunt after the landing of the First Fleet in 1788; other groups were not as directly affected until later. This guide uses the term 'Aboriginal' to speak broadly about colonial and frontier violence and the Stolen Generations, but *The Yield* is strongly about Wiradjuri experience. The following sections cover general information, and then specifically discuss Wiradjuri history. The reference section at the end of this guide provides more specific sources on Wiradjuri language and culture, including works by Wiradjuri writers.

The history wars

In the late 1990s, a public debate sometimes called the history wars emerged in Australia. Broadly speaking, the two sides differed on the question of whether the colonisation of Australia by Great Britain was primarily a humane endeavour, with the harmful consequences for Aboriginal Australians (such as death from infectious diseases) being largely unintentional; or whether it was marked by violent frontier wars with deliberate genocidal actions that have had long-term consequences. Those who favoured the former interpretation sometimes accused those who supported the latter of adopting a 'black armband' view of history.

Although some people still maintain that colonisation was humane and beneficial, most historians now recognise that there was widespread frontier violence. Researchers at the University of Newcastle, for example, have produced *Colonial Frontier Massacres, 1788 to 1930*, an interactive map that not only shows widespread violence but also indicates the relative recency of some of the events. Researchers also acknowledge that other colonial actions, including the removal of children from their families and the suppression of Aboriginal cultural practices and languages, were traumatic and have ongoing effects. Nor is this situation unique to Australia: in the United States, for example, Indigenous people were also removed from their land and had their cultures and languages suppressed, and the term 'First Nations' is sometimes used to indicate a commonality of experiences in colonised lands.

Aboriginal writers and researchers have produced a number of books designed to counteract colonial narratives about Aboriginal culture and history. (Such work has been done for many years; the following books are some important recent examples.) Perhaps the best known of these is *Dark Emu* (2014) by Bunurong and Yuin man Bruce Pascoe, which won several awards and has been widely discussed. *Dark Emu* is a strong influence on *The Yield*, as Winch acknowledges in her Acknowledgements, and makes a significant case for rethinking colonial understandings of the ways in which Aboriginal people managed the land prior to colonisation, including the importance of farming, grain harvesting and fishing. Academic and Kamilaroi woman Larissa Behrendt's *Finding Eliza: Power and Colonial Storytelling* (2016) examines the specific effects of colonisation on Aboriginal women, especially the ways in which missing Aboriginal girls and women are often overlooked by the media. There are echoes of this in *The Yield*, in Jedda's disappearance and the town's reaction.

More recently, a number of books by Aboriginal writers for younger readers have been published, including *Young Dark Emu: A Truer History* by Bruce Pascoe, Martu woman Karen Wyld's *Heroes, Rebels, and Innovators: Inspiring Aboriginal and Torres Strait Islander People from History* (2021), and Kamilaroi man Corey Tutt's *The First Scientists: Deadly Inventions and Innovations from Australia's First Peoples* (2021). It is important to recognise that these books do not present entirely *new* information, but rather provide perspectives and details that have been overlooked or deliberately repressed in colonial thinking.

Removals and the Stolen Generations

As we can see from Albert's experience, missions and children's homes played a key role in removing Aboriginal people from their families, cultures and countries. AIATSIS (Australian Institute of Aboriginal and Torres Strait Islander Studies) identifies missions, reserves and stations as the three spaces specifically constructed by the state and territory governments for housing Aboriginal people. Generally speaking, missions were church-run organisations, with a focus on converting people to Christianity; stations (also called 'managed reserves') were government-managed spaces, tightly controlled, whose managers had total control over their residents; and reserves (also called 'unmanaged reserves') were spaces set aside for Aboriginal people but not subject to direct government control. Prosperous House is first part of a mission, then part of a station ('the Mission church turned farm workers' quarters', p.40).

The removal of Aboriginal people to missions and homes was designed specifically to break cultural ties. People housed in missions spoke English rather than their own language, were isolated from other Aboriginal people, and were often separated from their family members. Children could be sent out to work (usually in domestic service for girls and stock work for boys, and often unpaid) or even adopted by white families. The Stolen Generations resulted from a succession of government acts that gave wide-ranging control to people usually called the Protector of Aborigines (the title varied from state to state), who would serve as guardian to Aboriginal children in the state. The process of removing Aboriginal children from their families was sometimes said to stem from a belief, at the time, that Aboriginal cultures and people were dying out: Australian colonial literature of this period often talks about Aboriginal Australians as a 'dying race', to justify the forcible assimilation of Aboriginal people into 'Australian' society. In fact, the removals exacerbated the devastation of Aboriginal cultures and languages, and caused ongoing trauma for families. At the same time, the missions became an important part of many people's stories, as *The Yield* indicates in its description of people returning to Prosperous House, seeking memories of their childhoods at the Mission and station.

In May 1997, a report on the Stolen Generations was tabled in Federal Parliament. Widely known as *Bringing Them Home*, and more formally as the *Report of the National Inquiry into the Separation of Aboriginal and Torres Strait Islander Children from Their Families*, the report was a response to concern among Aboriginal and Torres Strait Islander groups that the general public was not aware of the widespread nature of child removal. The push for recognition was supported by then prime minister Paul Keating's 'Redfern speech' (delivered in 1992), which publicly acknowledged the violence of colonialism and the removal of children from their families. Aboriginal groups had also been seeking accounts from separated mothers and children. For example, in 1995 the Aboriginal Legal Service of Western Australia published *Telling Our Story: A Report by the Aboriginal Legal Service of Western Australia (Inc) on the Removal of Aboriginal Children from Their Families in Western Australia*.

One consequence of the Stolen Generations was widespread damage to family ties, which in turn affected the continuation of culture and language. Albert's relationships with his ancestors in *The Yield*, for example, are central to his understanding of his own culture and language, but he also talks about being unable to 'find' his mother when he time travels, because she has been so traumatised by her experiences. Similarly, although he writes his dictionary, the account of him recording the words describes him as 'trying as he did to work out or remember how they were pronounced' (p.306). The process of recovery – as far as recovery is possible – from longstanding, wideranging and devastating government policies is an incomplete and ongoing one.

Wiradjuri history

Wiradjuri Country is central New South Wales, a vast area rich in land animals (including kangaroos and possums) and aquatic life (such as fish and yabbies). Wiradjuri man Lawrence Bamblett writes: 'The Wiradjuri nation, bordered by high mountain ranges in the east, spreads across rich valleys in an area of New South Wales roughly twice the size of the United Kingdom' (Bamblett 2013, p.40). He is drawing here on the work of Wiradjuri historians Mary Coe and Iris Clayton, who have produced important works such as Coe's *Windradyne: A Wiradjuri Koorie* (1986, illustrated by Isabel Coe) and Clayton's *Wiradjuri of the Rivers and Plains* (1997).

Rich, fertile land, however, was also attractive to the colonists, who made their way into Wiradjuri Country after crossing the Blue Mountains in 1813. As Stephen Gapps sets out in detail in *Gudyarra: The First Wiradyuri War of Resistance* (2021), Wiradjuri people met the invasion of their Country with strong opposition under the leadership of warriors such as Windradyne, who led the resistance until his death in 1829. Indeed, so intense was resistance that Gapps' book only covers what he calls the 'first Wiradyuri war of resistance' between 1822 and 1824, a period in which Governor Thomas Brisbane (Governor of New South Wales between 1821 and 1825) declared martial law 'west of the Blue Mountains' – that is, across Wiradjuri Country (Gapps 2021, p.5). Albert discusses this war in his dictionary: *nadhadirrambanhi* (pp.31–2).

Despite the resistance of warriors such as Windradyne, by the 1840s white colonisers were established along the Lachlan and Murrumbidgee Rivers, and the role of Protector of Aborigines was established. Missions and schools were also established, including Erambie Mission, the subject of Bamblett's *Our Stories Are Our Survival* (2013). Erambie, he notes, 'distinguished itself as an important site where the Wiradjuri confronted the inequalities of life in the mission era. Most importantly, it was a place where kinship ties were retained – and continues to be' (Bamblett 2013, p.42). While not denying the inequalities, Bamblett's description indicates the strength of Wiradjuri culture. Similarly, living Wiradjuri culture is apparent throughout *The Yield*, from Albert's feasts of bogong moths with his ancestors (p.255) to Elsie 'picking yam daisies for dinner' from the garden at Prosperous House (p.308).

However, although Wiradjuri people worked to retain kinship ties and culture, a great deal was lost during the violent dispossession. As a result of removals and bans on speech, Wiradjuri language has been considered functionally extinct. However, it has been subject to a long-term revival process, led largely by Wiradjuri Elder Stan Grant Senior and John Rudder, a researcher who specialises in Aboriginal languages. For more information on Wiradjuri language, see the 'Language' section, below. A publication edited by Wiradjuri writer Anita Heiss, *Growing Up Wiradjuri* (2022), includes the memories and life stories of eight Wiradjuri elders, a concept not dissimilar to Albert's dictionary. These reclamation narratives reinforce the fact that Wiradjuri culture is still living and active despite the lasting impact of colonial violence and trauma.

GENRE, STRUCTURE & LANGUAGE

Genre

The Yield falls into the category of literary fiction, which (broadly speaking) is fiction that does not fit within a specific genre: for instance, it is not romance, or science fiction, or historical fiction. Nevertheless, literary fiction has its own generic features. It is sometimes said that while 'genre' fiction relies on plot, 'literary' fiction relies on character, and it is true that strong, fully realised characters are at least as central to *The Yield* as the plot is.

In practice, the distinctions between 'literary' fiction and 'genre' fiction are often less significant than the similarities: each can rely equally on complex characters, strong plots and realistic world-building. *The Yield* plays with features that might otherwise be associated with genre fiction, including Albert's time travel and his conversations with his ancestors, August's strong flashbacks to her childhood through traumatic memory (one of which, during Albert's funeral, is presented almost as a bodily transfer into the past), and Jedda's existence in the brolga. However, it is important to note that all these events are presented quite literally and factually in the novel, and not as part of a speculative world. As such, the novel does not quite fit the scope of what is sometimes called 'magic realism', a genre in which an otherwise realistic setting is affected by supernatural events: Albert, Missy, August and the other characters in *The Yield* accept events such as Albert's time travel as absolutely real and concrete, not as paranormal.

A number of contemporary Australian novels examine colonisation and its impact on Aboriginal Australians. Two of the better-known ones, which have also been adapted for film and television, are Kate Grenville's *The Secret River* (2005) and Craig Silvey's *Jasper Jones* (2009). However, both are written by white Australian authors, so their perspective and narrative focus is that of white Australia. Wiradjuri author and academic Jeanine Leane undertook what she called a 'tracking' of Aboriginal representation in such 'settler nation writing' in 2014, and her essay is a vital resource for thinking about how writing is also rewriting: 'All these novels', Leane writes of white Australian stories, 'are set in *places*; not just empty spaces, they are named already by the original inhabitants and then renamed by contact, overwritten' (Leane 2014).

It is important, therefore, to put *The Yield* in the context of other works by Aboriginal Australian authors, including Anita Heiss' *Bila Yarrudhanggalangdhuray* (2021), which is set on Wiradjuri Country in the mid-nineteenth century; Jeanine Leane's *Purple Threads* (2011), a collection of short stories about rural Wiradjuri life in the twentieth century; Julie Janson's novel *Benevolence* (2020), which is told from the perspective of a Darug woman born in the early years of the colony; Melissa Lucashenko's *Too Much Lip* (2018), about the planned development of a river on Bundjalung Country sacred to a local family; Alexis Wright's wide-ranging novel of the precarious settlements in the Top End, *Carpentaria* (2006); and Kim Scott's *That Deadman Dance* (2010), which recounts early encounters between Noongar people and colonisers in Western Australia. (Like *The Yield*, both *Too Much Lip* and *That Deadman Dance* won the Miles Franklin Literary Award.)

Structure

The Yield has a cyclical structure, beginning and ending with the word *Ngurambang* (Country). Albert says that he is writing his dictionary backwards, which he is, from a purely alphabetical perspective, but he is also writing it forwards, since he unravels some mysteries, such as the disappearance of Jedda and the murder of Jimmy. The alphabetical structure is imposed by the English words for which he is providing the Wiradjuri equivalents.

The Yield uses first-person and third-person narratives. Albert and Rev. Greenleaf narrate in the first person, and Rev. Greenleaf's narrative is further complicated by being a letter written for a specific recipient, Dr George Cross of the British Society of Ethnography, whom the reader never meets. The third-person narrative focuses on August Gondiwindi. While a third-person perspective can allow the reader to know the thoughts of multiple characters, the third-person sections of *The Yield* only really describe August's thoughts, although the reader can infer the thoughts and feelings of some other main characters.

The novel also has a nested structure of narratives within narratives. It begins and ends with Albert Gondiwindi's first-person narrative, which surrounds both the third-person narrative of August Gondiwindi and the first-person narrative of Rev. Greenleaf. This latter narrative is particularly significant. In some ways Rev. Greenleaf is writing against his own time's prevailing ideas about Aboriginal people. While he is paternalistic and participates in the removal of family members, he is also sympathetic and open to differing knowledges. At the same time, his is a conventional point of view: he is a white Australian writing about Aboriginal people, absorbing their own history, experiences, names and language from his own Western viewpoint. Note, for example, the difference in the way he and Albert spell Baymee (p.152) / Biyaami, Baiame (p.253), and Albert lists other examples of words that Rev. Greenleaf has, probably unwittingly, Anglicised. Although Greenleaf is sympathetic to the Aboriginal people he knows and cares for, he is translating, reinterpreting and ultimately distorting their experiences; in other words, he is part of the colonial process. But by enclosing his narrative within Albert's, Winch makes Albert's the framing narrative and the overarching perspective, and reclaims Aboriginal experiences, languages and perspectives.

The Yield also incorporates elements of epistolary fiction in Rev. Greenleaf's serial letter, written for Dr George Cross and later published in a newspaper (p.304). The letter is written during a period of internment, first on Torrens Island (in the Port River Estuary near

Adelaide) and later at Holsworthy Internment Camp (in Sydney); these camps held men of German and Austro-Hungarian heritage during World War I, when Australia was at war with Germany and such men were considered possible spies or enemy combatants. The narrative advantage of epistolary fiction – which consists largely or entirely of letters – is that it allows for multiple narrative perspectives. In this case, the third-person narrative focused on August is combined with Rev. Greenleaf's historical first-person narrative, as well as Albert's iconoclastic dictionary, also narrated in the first person. This combination of narratives provides the reader with an individual perspective on colonisation (and on guilt and shame) from the point of view of a coloniser, knowledge of family secrets known only to Albert Gondiwindi, and an understanding of August's mind and memories.

Language

Language, particularly the Wiradjuri language, is at the core of *The Yield*. Albert's dictionary stands as a reaction to the widespread loss of Aboriginal languages as a result of colonisation. This loss of language was due especially to the forced removal of children from their families and the impact of missions and mission schools, which enforced the use of English and suppressed Indigenous languages, as well as the removal of Aboriginal people from the Country on which their language was spoken.

Language is significant in the novel in a number of ways. As Winch indicates through Albert's dictionary, language has a key role to play in maintaining and sharing culture. Language is shaped by cultural practices: how certain words or phrases develop is the result of behaviours and beliefs. For example, when the authorities consider the Gondiwindis' Native Title application, they do not only look at the land itself (e.g. the fish traps) or artefacts at the museum for evidence of farming practices: 'The evidence of their civilisation, after so many years of farming, was difficult to find on the surface of the land. But they said it was embedded in Albert's dictionary' (p.307). Albert also makes this point at the beginning of the novel when he says, 'The dictionary is not just words – there are little stories in those pages too' (p.11). The final words of August's narrative are: 'Better these words and better we are still here and that we speak them' (p.310). In other words, the existence of language itself (in a dictionary, for instance) is not enough, because it also needs to be spoken and shared.

The Wiradjuri language has been subject to an extensive revitalisation process, whereby the language is brought back into everyday use for a new generation of speakers. Wiradjuri Elder Stan Grant Senior has worked on the continuation and revival of Wiradjuri language for many years. With academic John Rudder, he published *Wiradjuri Language Songs for Children of All Ages* (1998) and *Wiradjuri Language Colouring in Book* (1998), and he has continued to work on the revitalisation of this language. The work of both men is credited in the Acknowledgements section of *The Yield* (p.343). The significance of this work is reflected in the fact that people can now obtain a Graduate Certificate in Wiradjuri Language, Culture and Heritage from Charles Sturt University, which in turn has a broad-reaching effect on the revitalisation of all aspects of Wiradjuri culture.

CHAPTER-BY-CHAPTER ANALYSIS

Chapters 1–3 (pp.1–12)

Summary: *Albert 'Poppy' Gondiwindi outlines his plan to write a dictionary following a terminal diagnosis; August Gondiwindi learns of Albert's death; Albert defines yarran tree / spearwood tree.*

The opening chapter sets out some of the novel's core ideas.

- The value of language: 'Every person around should learn the word for *country* in the old language, the first language – because that is the way to all time, to time travel!' (p.1).
- The impact of colonisation on Aboriginal people: 'So in a country where we weren't really allowed to be, I decided to *be*' (pp.1–2).
- The interrelationship of memory and story: 'I am writing because the spirits are urging me to remember, and because the town needs to know that I remember, they need to know now more than ever before' (p.2).
- The relative nature of time: Albert talks about his death in terms of having 'the church time against me' (p.3), but he also positions the concept of 'deep time' against this linear model of time. 'The big stuff goes forever, time ropes and loops and is never straight, that's the real story of time' (p.2).

Albert is part of the Stolen Generations. As a child, he was escorted to the Mission by 'police officers on horses' (p.5), and then separated from his mother and his younger sister. The novel balances this with a description of Albert in his 'final hours' (p.5).

Albert emphasises that he is writing his dictionary backwards, beginning with 'y' since 'we don't have a Z word in our alphabet' (p.12). The dictionary also moves backwards conceptually: Albert mentions that he 'once made a spear in order to kill a man' (p.12), but the story of the spear and the killing does not unfold until later in the novel. Similarly, August's story is hinted at in Chapter 2 when she feels that 'the worst thing that could ever happen had already happened' (p.8). The reader does not find out until much later how this 'worst thing' and Albert's spearing a man are related.

Key vocabulary

Black rhino: a species of rhinoceros. Three subspecies of black rhinos have been declared extinct, most recently the western black rhino, declared extinct in 2011.

Deep time: sometimes called *geologic time*, a concept that encompasses the geologic history of the planet. Albert's positioning of deep time against 'church time' is significant, as the theories of deep time developed during the eighteenth century were in conflict with the church's position on the biblical age of the earth. In Albert's case, deep time and church time mirror Aboriginal custodianship of Country and white Australia's colonisation of the land.

Q What is the effect of telling the story backwards?

Chapters 4–5 (pp.13–26)

Summary: *August returns home to Prosperous House after being away for ten years; Albert defines more 'y' words.*

The placenames in *The Yield* are elemental: City Highway, Hinterland Highway, Broken Highway, Massacre Plains. The further August travels from the urban centre (Sydney), the more abstract the names become, representing not only the drought-stricken landscape but also the colonial violence in which it is steeped. The narrative sums up the townspeople's limited opportunities: 'Some made do on unemployment benefits and some had jobs though few had careers' (p.14).

Because August has been absent for so long, she is able to look at Prosperous House as though she is almost a stranger, and the narrative depicts the landscape as August sees it, both familiar and yet unfamiliar (see particularly pages 16–18).

Key vocabulary

Lutheran rose: the symbol of the Lutheran Church; a white rose with a red centre containing a black cross.

Q What is the distinction Winch is making between having a job and having a career?

Q What role does Christianity play in *The Yield*? (See also Albert's definition of *dulbi-nya* on p.41.)

Key point

Although this specific Massacre Plains is a fictional place, Winch's note at the end of the novel emphasises that Massacre and Poisoned Waterhole Creek are actual Australian placenames. The name recalls ways in which the sites of massacres and colonial violence are recorded by First Nations people. For example, filmmaker Rachel Perkins visits a site called 'Blackfellow's Bones' on Arrernte Country in the documentary series *The Australian Wars* (2022), and shares a recording of her grandmother's testimony about the massacre there.

Chapters 6–7 (pp.27–35)

Summary: *August spends a sleepless night at Prosperous House; Albert defines 'w' words, including 'war' and 'where is your country?'*

Chapter 6 contains August's memories of how grief has affected both the family and the town. Whereas Albert and Elsie had always been active in the community – holding karate classes, for example – and workers came to stay on the property, all of this ceased when Jedda disappeared. Parents became more active in tracking their children, meeting them at bus stops and preventing them from playing in the street. But Jedda's disappearance actually increased the sense of separation between the Gondiwindis and the rest of the town. Gondiwindi children were not included in the fears of other parents, who 'never double-checked if they saw a Gondiwindi walking home alone' (p.28), and even the news reports were brief. This situation is echoed in the other ways in which violence against Aboriginal people is ignored, which Rev. Greenleaf's narrative describes in more detail.

In Chapter 7 Albert's dictionary reinforces the family's custodianship of Country: the Gondiwindi were 'farmers and fishermen and they cultivated the land here long before' (p.31), the ancestors told Albert 'about all the plants and trees and how to use them' (p.32), and the Gondiwindi 'had their own flours, and they were meant especially for the body of the Gondiwindi' (p.33).

The names August recalls on page 28 – 'the Coes, Gibsons, Grants' – are real names; the work of Stan Grant Senior and of Mary and Isabel Coe is referred to in the 'Wiradjuri history' section on pages 10–11 of this guide. This section also has information about war, relevant to Albert's entry on page 31 of *The Yield*.

Key vocabulary

Paterson's curse: an invasive plant species, reportedly brought to Australia by Jane Paterson, a settler in the regional New South Wales town of Albury.

Q What does Winch mean when she says that Jedda 'became a mystery manufactured to forget about' (p.28)?

Q How is the account of Jedda's disappearance similar to real-life cases, such as the Bowraville disappearances?

Chapters 8–10 (pp.37–51)

Summary: *August's childhood and her parents' arrest are described; Albert defines 'w', 'u', 't', and 's' words; the first instalment of Ferdinand Greenleaf's serial letter describes his purpose in writing.*

August remembers key elements of her childhood: the early stages of her eating disorder (a compulsion to eat, rather than her current compulsion to starve), her parents' unemployment and emotional instability, the ways in which she and Jedda had relied on each other, and the ultimate breaking up of the home.

August thinks of the return to Prosperous House as the moment 'their lives had become best-case scenarios' but she also regards the place as 'five hundred acres of not being able to shake the past, of where everything had gone wrong, over and over' (p.40). This is a central conflict in the novel: Country as a source of nurturing and belonging, but also as a site of colonial violence and ongoing trauma. Rev. Greenleaf's serial letter, which begins at this point of the novel, provides significant context for what 'everything had gone wrong, over and over' means for the Gondiwindi.

Key vocabulary

British Society of Ethnography: this specific organisation is likely fictional, but reflects real organisations, such as the Royal Anthropological Institute of Great Britain and Ireland (established in 1843).

Ethnography: the scientific description of people and cultures; the field of ethnography is a subset of anthropology.

Skjold: a real ship; the *Skjold* was a three-mast Danish barque, which arrived in Port Adelaide on 28 October 1841 from Altona in Germany.

Q Could *The Yield* have told the same story without Rev. Greenleaf's letter? Justify your answer.

Chapters 11–13 (pp.53–81)

Summary: *August remembers her first years at Prosperous House; she meets her old friend, Eddie Falstaff, and her aunties; she learns about the mine; Ferdinand Greenleaf recounts his childhood arrival in Australia and his plan to start a mission; Albert defines more 's' words.*

Chapter 11 refers to several events that become more significant later: Great Aunt Mary's down-turned mouth (p.60, referencing 'the bad in her own son' – Uncle Jimmy – and his death), and the pharmacy in town that burnt down (p.58, referencing Joey's arrest).

When Rev. Greenleaf critiques the treatment of 'the Natives – *mere children!*' (p.70), he is partly talking about the indentured servitude of Aboriginal children from boys' and girls' homes. But the phrase also recalls the paternalistic attitude of even sympathetic colonial figures, who denied the sophistication of Aboriginal society. Although less graphic than the violence Greenleaf later describes, this paternalism also plays a role in the ongoing trauma and disenfranchisement of Aboriginal people.

Key vocabulary

'Men love darkness …': a quote from John 3:19, the same chapter of the Bible as 'For God so loved the world …' (John 3:16).

S116: a section of the Australian constitution that protects religious freedom. It has been used in Native Title claims to argue that mining concessions granted without the permission of Native Title holders impair the exercise of traditional Aboriginal spirituality.

Sesquicentenary: the 150th anniversary of an event – in this case, the 1788 arrival of the First Fleet. The sesquicentenary, marked on 26 January 1938, was notable for being the first national protest gathering of Aboriginal people, and is known as the Day of Mourning.

St Jude: the patron saint of lost causes and desperate situations.

Those who had escaped religious persecution from Prussia and Germany: sometimes called the Old Lutherans, this group refused to join the Prussian Union of Churches and emigrated in large numbers in the 1830s and 1840s to Australia, Canada and the United States.

Q 'But in every mobile-library book, she could never find herself or her sister. Never a girl like August or Jedda Gondiwindi, not ever' (p.62). What is the meaning of these sentences?

Q Why does August feel that she 'hadn't given the time of day to the sorrow they'd meant to be united by' (p.67)?

Key point

The highly offensive and outdated terms 'quadroon', 'octoroon' and 'half-caste', used by settlers throughout *The Yield* (and present in Albert's recollection on page 77), reflect an ongoing obsession with blood: not just the spilling of blood (as Missy later talks about in the museum) but also the measuring and quantifying of blood, and the connection, in colonial thinking, between blood and culture. This notion (sometimes called 'blood quantum') is not part of the Gondiwindis' perspective, but one imposed from outside. See 'Different interpretations' for further discussion of blood in *The Yield*.

Chapters 14–16 (pp.83–108)

Summary: *August travels into town and helps Elsie pack up Prosperous House; Rev. Greenleaf begins the Mission; Albert defines 's', 'r', 'q' and 'p' words.*

August's visit to the town emphasises its poverty: the streets are empty, although people watch from windows (p.85), the real estate agency itself is for sale (p.85) and the Aboriginal Medical Centre and Land Council is closed and empty (pp.86–7). The only bright and well-tended area is the war memorial, the grass of which is watered (despite the drought) and trimmed (p.86). This reinforces why the mine is popular – it will bring employment and life back into the region – and why the town is vulnerable to the mining company's approach. It also hints at a town that glorifies its past, instead of grappling with the present-day consequences of that past.

The contents of Prosperous House are being packed up because Elsie is moving, and there are echoes in this process of the removal and wrapping of Jedda's photos (p.27), which in turn hints at the taboo in some Aboriginal communities that prevents the use of names and images of people who have died.

Rev. Greenleaf's narrative suggests some of the ways in which Aboriginal communities were curtailed while living on the Mission. For example, he allows Mission residents to visit the town but 'not to engage with the political discussions over Corroboree', because 'the neighbouring Natives like to gather during blanket distribution, each May, to persuade each other to demand autonomy' (p.99). These actions contribute to the breaking of cultural and community ties. Albert's emphasis on the importance of songlines (p.103) reinforces this. (See also Albert's more sinister reference to blankets on pages 262–3 for further context.)

Key vocabulary

Freedom Ride: a trip taken in 1965 by a group called the Student Action for Aborigines (students from Sydney University), which travelled into country New South Wales on fact-finding missions to learn about the lives of Aboriginal people; they also protested about segregated areas, including pools.

Songlines: lines or routes in a landscape that have associated oral histories as well as stories of creation and ancestors; often connected to ceremonial and sacred sites.

Q What does Elsie mean when she says, 'You can't ask hungry folks to go on a hunger strike' (p.94)?

Chapters 17–19 (pp.109–28)

Summary: *August visits Eddie and begins preparations for Albert's funeral; Rev. Greenleaf deals with violence at the Mission; Albert defines 'p', 'o' and 'm' words.*

August's reunion with Eddie is fraught, in part because they have not met for ten years, and in part because of Eddie's unthinking sense of privilege – evident, for instance, when he casually jokes, 'You're a British subject even if you're a Gondi' (p.111). This chapter also contains the first indications that Eddie feels trapped at Massacre Plains, that his sense (or possibly his parents' sense) of responsibility for the land is not Albert's deeply entrenched custodianship, but more of a prison (p.111).

Elsie's memories of Albert and his family are also tinged with disturbing undercurrents, as in 'Aunt Betty and Aunt Nora [...] who'd grown up with Poppy and then without Poppy, at and then away from the Station' (p.113) and Elsie's account of Albert's cousin Fred, who amputated his own hand after failing to get medical care (p.117). While Eddie is frustrated by the fact that his privilege comes with strict boundaries, the undercurrents in Albert's family are more about the experience of trauma, especially from the breaking of family ties.

Rev. Greenleaf records the birth of Mercy in 1881: Mercy is the mother of Augustine, and Albert's grandmother, which reinforces the family's close ties to the Mission (p.119). But his narrative also highlights how the Mission is built on ignoring or breaking existing family ties. For example, Greenleaf sends Daisy away after she is raped, although her family is 'quite distressed at this' (p.122).

Q What narrative relationship is there between Eddie's jokes and Rev. Greenleaf's stories of violence at the Mission?

Chapters 20–2 (pp.129–60)

Summary: *August meets the mine protestors; Albert's funeral begins; Rev. Greenleaf takes the advice of Aboriginal people on fishing and farming; Albert defines 'm', 'l', 'k', 'j' and 'i' words.*

August's walking along the dry bed of the Murrumby is also (as with Albert's walks around the farm) a form of time travel, a walking back. She sees the mussel middens and the remains of the fish traps: both indicate long-term occupation and farming of the land, so can protect against mining claims and work in favour of Native Title applications. The possibility of making a Native Title claim is raised when August is talking to her cousin Joey, who had spoken to Albert about putting in a claim (p.142). Aunt Nicki also mentions 'scar trees', the carved trees that have ritual meaning and can play a part in a claim (p.146).

These forms of connection to the land are reinforced by Rev. Greenleaf's narrative, which contrasts the reliability of Aboriginal fishing and farming practices with the Mission's failed harvest, withered 'from the sheer violence of the sun' (p.150).

August's meeting with Mandy, one of the protesters (pp.134–7), recalls Albert's definition of 'where is your country?' in Chapter 7.

Missy's story of Albert taking his daughters fishing (pp.140–1) comes to have a different significance when we later learn that his 'fishing' late in life is largely a way of searching for Jedda's body.

Key vocabulary

Baiame: a creator figure in the Dreaming of several nations across south-eastern Australia, including that of the Wiradjuri people. Rev. Greenleaf's spelling, *Baymee* (p.152), reflects both his efforts to understand Wiradjuri culture and his inability to grasp it completely.

Mabo: Eddie Koiki Mabo, a Torres Strait Islander man whose landmark land rights claim – *Mabo v Queensland (No.2)* – was central to overturning the false doctrine of terra nullius.

Q What does Chapter 20 indicate, firstly, about what is needed for a Native Title claim, and secondly, about the difficulties in applying for one?

Q What does Albert mean by, 'So I never reached for an easy fix. I just tried' (p.156)?

Chapters 23–5 (pp.161–78)

Summary: *Albert's funeral is held; the Mission is attacked by a group of six white men; Albert defines 'h' words.*

The brolga that appears at Albert's funeral is connected to key moments earlier in the novel's time frame.

- August's memory of 'Jedda as she took his arm when he went to run his hand through August's hair' (p.163) recalls an event leading up to Jedda's death.

- The refrain of *'Heads, shoulders, knees and toes'* that marks the brolga's dance (p.164) recalls Aunt Nicki's memory of Albert using that song to try to keep language alive for the children (p.146).
- The presence of the brolga and the memory it evokes brings language back to August, in the word *burrul-gang*: 'She didn't know how she knew the word but she knew it' (p.167).

Rev. Greenleaf mentions the 'cemetery that had been swelling in size, growing with the suffering that hung like a pall of locusts over the plains' (p.173): this becomes significant at the end of the novel.

Key vocabulary

Brolga: a bird in the crane family, well known for its mating dance.

Q What types of animals appear throughout *The Yield*? What is their significance?

Key point

Jedda (also known as *Jedda the Uncivilized*) is a 1955 film by Australian filmmaker Charles Chauvel. Aboriginal girl Jedda is adopted as an infant by a white woman living on a remote Northern Territory cattle station, whose own child has died. Forbidden to have contact with the Aboriginal people who live on the station, she finds herself increasingly drawn to them as she grows up. As in other texts of this time, the film presents an Aboriginal person living in a white society as being torn between two worlds (much as August, moving to England in the wake of Jedda's disappearance, finds herself at home in neither world). The film was significant for its time, but does reproduce colonial assumptions about Aboriginal people and culture.

Chapters 26–8 (pp.179–207)

Summary: *August looks for Albert's missing manuscript and retraces his steps at the library; Rev. Greenleaf prepares for the Chicago World's Fair; Albert defines 'h', 'g', 'f', and 'e' words.*

After the funeral, the 'cement block of her memory ... cracked' (p.164) and August's memories of Jedda become much stronger; touching their old toys evokes rich sensory childhood memories.

Rev. Greenleaf's letter recounts two kinds of violence: one explicit and one implicit. The massacres he refers to are part of continuing frontier violence, and the activities of the Protection Board lead to a violent division of families, creating the Stolen Generations. But the removal of Wowhely's spear to the museum, beginning the process of collection, is also a form of colonial violence and trauma. August's tactile use of toys and other objects to evoke memories suggests what has been lost as a result of the Falstaffs' donations of Gondiwindi artefacts to the museum, removing a physical connection with memory and culture. Albert's dictionary reinforces this when the ancestors show him the remnants of the stringybark homes being ploughed into the fields (p.203).

The library, like the museum, is a form of gatekeeping (see the key point on page 32 of this guide for a discussion of gatekeeping). August's encounters with two very different librarians indicate the ways in which knowledge can be either locked away or freely shared. Albert's dictionary also touches on this (p.127).

Key vocabulary

Agro's Cartoon Connection: a children's television program that aired from 1990 to 1997. The program was primarily a vehicle for showing cartoons, connected by brief studio segments starring the puppet Agro.

Human zoo: public displays of so-called 'primitive' peoples, generally presenting marginalised groups as 'savages' while upholding the perceived superiority of Western civilisation. Organised protests against human zoos became more common in the early twentieth century, but they continued in the same form until as late as the 1958 World's Fair in Brussels.

Mother Goose: a talking toy, first produced in 1986. The toy played stories on cassette tape, and included an accompanying book so that children could read along with the stories.

World's Fair: World's Fairs were held from 1791 onwards; the 1893 Chicago World's Fair marked the 400th anniversary of Christopher Columbus' arrival in the New World. The 1893 fair prompted protests from civil rights leaders about segregation and the exclusion of African Americans. Chicago is also a site of dislocation for Native American people, who were forcibly removed after the 1833 Treaty of Chicago.

Q What is the significance of the 1893 World's Fair to the narrative of *The Yield*, particularly given its connection to Christopher Columbus?

Key point

Albert's books (p.187) represent different ways of approaching Australian history, which converge on the Prosperous Mission. *A History of Australia* is one of the central settler accounts of Australian history, a six-volume history of Australia from 1788 to 1945; *The Story of the Australian Church* balances the secular histories of Australia with a religious history; *A Million Wild Acres* tells Australia's history through a consideration of the settlers' impact on the landscape; *Cooper's Creek* is a nonfiction account of the Burke and Wills expedition into Australia's interior; *The Fatal Impact* explores, as the subtitle states, 'the invasion of the South Pacific', concentrating particularly on Captain James Cook; and *Blood on the Wattle* covers massacres and other destructive effects of colonisation on Aboriginal Australians since 1788.

Chapters 29–32 (pp.209–28)

Summary: *August visits Eddie, and an ill-fated sexual encounter leads to him revealing that his family has sent Gondiwindi artefacts to the museum; Albert defines 'e' and 'd' words; Rev. Greenleaf is registered as an illegal alien after the outbreak of World War I before being interned; Albert defines 'c' words.*

August's encounter with Eddie reveals both the positive and negative aspects of being tied to a place. For August, although she has been running away from Prosperous for a long time, it has been 'a place I could always come back to' (p.217). For Eddie, although his position is one of great privilege, his connection to the land is less positive and more entrapping; he feels as though he is the only one who cannot leave (p.217). Part of his lashing out at August and his revelation that his family has been giving Gondiwindi artefacts to the museum for decades is a desire to disrupt her connection to the land, as his feels disrupted. It is also a continuation of his casually racist comment from Chapter 17: now, when he tells August, 'This is where all your culture is! Under fucking glass!' (p.219), he is much more explicit about his relationship to the local Aboriginal people.

Eddie's violence and the rapacity (greed) of his ancestors are reflected in Rev. Greenleaf's references to the rising nationalism in the years leading up to World War I, and the antagonism towards Australians of German origin. Each situation involves a repositioning of what it means to be Australian, and who is allowed to be Australian. This issue recurs in Chapter 33, when the man with the Southern Cross tattoo talks to August about who belongs and who does not (p.237). In Rev. Greenleaf's case, he has seen his sense of belonging shift across his lifetime: from the hardworking German immigrants who spoke only English and Anglicised their surname, to the German-Australians deemed to be a threat in time of war. Belonging is not fixed, but shifts depending on who has power.

Q What effect does Rev. Greenleaf's fate have on the message conveyed by the novel as a whole?

Chapters 33–4 (pp.229–56)

Summary: *August tells Aunt Missy about the artefacts and they visit the library; the librarian offers to email August a PDF of Rev. Greenleaf's serialised letter; a mining official comes to the house; August and Missy drive to the city to visit the museum where the artefacts are held, reading Rev. Greenleaf's letter on the way; Albert defines 'b' words.*

While Albert 'spent his retirement on the upkeep of the garden and fishing at Lake Broken and along the full end of the Murrumby' (p.229), his dictionary makes it clear that he wasn't only trying to catch fish: 'I wasn't wading out to get a good catch, I was always looking for Jedda' (p.254). The fishing, which has been a bright memory at the funeral, is also tinged with trauma.

The fishing spear, the first item in the Falstaff Permanent Collection, is a nexus for various themes in the text, including frontier violence (since it was inherited after the murder of its owner, Wowhely) and the removal of culture and people. Ultimately, it represents a disjunction between living, continuous Aboriginal culture (as experienced by Albert, particularly through and with his ancestors) and the colonial treatment of it as a museum specimen, something to be collected, filed and archived rather than lived. Aunt Missy's comments about tokenism in Chapter 35 (pp.261–2) and August's sense of the museum as a cemetery (p.263) are developments of the ideas in this chapter.

As August sinks back into her family and culture (she follows Albert's research, learns about the artefacts, remembers language), some of the trauma she has been experiencing starts to lift: for example, she becomes hungry again (p.237).

After August reads out Rev. Greenleaf's letter, she asks Missy if she thinks the Reverend 'was kind' (p.250), but the novel suggests there is no easy answer. He stands against some forms of colonial violence (rape and murder, the chains as depicted in the museum), but he enacts other forms (the imposition of Christianity, the removal of children and sending of young women into domestic service, the erosion of culture and language). Increasingly, acts such as the suppression of language are recognised as forms of violence.

Key vocabulary

Milton: John Milton (1608–1674), an English poet, best known for his epic poem *Paradise Lost,* which recounts the temptation of Adam and Eve and their expulsion from Eden. He stated that the purpose of this work was to 'justifie the wayes of God to men'.

Q What is the significance of the indirect reference to a poem called *Paradise Lost* at this point in the novel (p.250)?

Q What does Aunt Missy mean by her statement, 'He [Rev. Greenleaf] was bad in a long pattern of bad' (p.250)?

Key point

The novel is full of examples of gatekeeping: in this context, situations in which barriers are placed between Aboriginal people and access to culture, community and knowledge. The museum and the Gondiwindi artefacts are the most explicit example of this, but the Mission itself is also an example of gatekeeping, as it removes Aboriginal people from their Country, culture and language, and imposes Christian beliefs and the English language. Albert's dictionary is a means of circumventing gatekeeping by restoring a language whose use was forbidden. As such, Joey and August's circulation of the dictionary among the town's children at the end of the novel is the opposite action to Albert and his mother walking to the Mission, escorted by police, in the opening pages.

Chapters 35–6 (pp.257–71)

Summary: *August and Aunt Missy visit the museum to see the Gondiwindi artefacts and return to find the mine has begun demolition; Rev. Greenleaf is incarcerated.*

Visiting the museum is a turning point for August: it connects to what she has been taught about her history ('those schoolbook lies', pp.26–7) and to Rev. Greenleaf's letter, so that 'she felt as if she'd awoken from a stony sleep to find herself standing on the edge of something larger than she'd ever been able to see before' (p.266). Rev. Greenleaf's narrative also touches on the idea of a history that is invisible or that has been erased: 'I fear my truth will go unnoticed' (p.269).

Missy's comment that people are 'so scared of not having everything … that our people are gunna have nothing' (p.266) resonates with the title of the novel, and with Albert's explanation of the idea of the yield (p.25) as being simultaneously what you can take from the land (in English) and what you can give to it (in Wiradjuri).

Q What is the significance of Albert speaking to Missy as she walks around the museum?

Q What is the connection between Missy's outburst at the museum (p.261) and Elsie's civil rights work as a young woman (pp.281–3)? How are these connected to the protest at the mining site?

Chapters 37–8 (pp.273–85)

Summary: *August realises what has happened to Albert's manuscript and goes to retrieve it; Albert defines 'a' words.*

The destruction of Prosperous House is a microcosm of the historical destruction visited on the land across the years. The future devastation the tin mine will cause, tearing up two kilometres of land, and the past massacres, sexual violence and separations, are all echoed in the burning and ploughing of the fields. Albert's dictionary reinforces this, with an emphasis on acts of segregation, separation and isolation.

Q What does Albert mean when he says Aboriginal people were 'together and isolated at once' (p.285)?

Chapters 39–42 (pp.287–312)

Summary: *August, Joey and Aunt Missy join the protest against the mine; Aunt Nicki arrives with Albert's book; Rev. Greenleaf's obituary is published; a cemetery is uncovered on the site of the old Mission; the family learns what happened to Jedda; August decides to stay in Massacre Plains; Albert defines more 'a' words.*

Mandy's emphasis on 'the nobody of everybody' (p.298) speaks to a sense of collective power: the focus should be on collective benefits rather than on individual greed (which the mine represents, since its primary purpose is the enriching of a small group, while the economic benefits to the town are secondary). There are traces of this idea in Albert's description of Gondiwindi farming and fire practices, in which all participate for the benefit of all (p.256). The fire lit by the protestors connects these ideas, as does Albert's definition of *ngumbaay-dyil* (all together in one place) in the previous chapter (pp.284–5). Aunt Missy's *Treaty* t-shirt (p.296) also connects this protest to previous (and ongoing) protests.

The protest is the culmination of August's slow process of sinking back into the land and of coming back to family, culture and herself, which has accelerated after the museum visit. On pages 301–2, she and the other protestors experience something of the time travel that Albert experienced.

The novel ultimately resists easy endings. August's and Jedda's stories reach a certain resolution, but the stories of the mine and the Native Title application are not concluded, which prevents the ending from feeling too neatly resolved.

Key vocabulary

Bernardo Bellotto: an Italian urban landscape painter (1721–1780). He was the court painter for King Stanislaus Augustus Poniatowski of Poland, for whom he painted many views of Warsaw.

Montaigne: Michel de Montaigne (1533–1592), a French philosopher.

Sachsen: known in English as Saxony, a German state. Saxony gives its name to the Saxons who, after migrating to Britain in the Dark Ages, emerged as the Anglo-Saxons. Rev. Greenleaf, then, is from the very heart of empire.

Vedute: highly detailed paintings of cityscapes; from the Italian word for 'view'.

Q What differences are there between the way the artefacts in the Falstaff Collection are presented and how the recording of Albert's dictionary is presented?

Q What is the significance of the *vedute* paintings (p.311)?

CHARACTERS & RELATIONSHIPS

Albert Gondiwindi

Key quotes

'Big thing, best thing she [Elsie] taught me was to learn to write the words too, taught me I wasn't just a second-rate man raised on white flour and Christianity.' (p.2)

'Dad had a good life [...] And a hard life, too.' (Aunt Missy, p.64)

A member of the Stolen Generations, Albert is removed from his mother at the age of three and raised in a boys' home; he later reconnects with his mother (p.255) and his sister Mary. His mother, Augustine, is the child of Mercy, one of the first children born at Rev. Greenleaf's Mission, so Albert's family is not only connected to Country but also has a long connection with the Mission. Augustine becomes an alcoholic, which Albert refers to as 'an Old World disease' (p.1), referencing the fact that alcohol was brought to Australia by colonists (and, as Rev. Greenleaf makes clear, used as a tool of violence).

Albert leaves the boys' home to work as a stockman, and later works as overseer of the seasonal workers at Prosperous House (p.43), the former Mission building, and farms the land; he lives there with his wife Elsie and their three daughters. He and Elsie run a wide range of activities for the local community: mothers' groups and needlework classes, Bible study and karate instruction, field and garden work, and Albert also escorts visitors 'on long walks around the property' (p.53). One of the consequences of Jedda's disappearance is that all of these extra activities cease, and Albert and Elsie withdraw from community life.

After a diagnosis of pancreatic cancer, Albert takes on the task of writing his dictionary 'because the spirits are urging me to remember, and because the town needs to know that I remember' (p.2). It is possible that he would have taken on this work regardless, since he discussed

Native Title with his grandson Joey (pp.142–3), but the work becomes more urgent with the combination of his diagnosis and the plans to create the tin mine.

August Gondiwindi

Key quotes

'When August was a little kid she couldn't rely on the certainty of even a day.' (p.308)

'She had ached for that thing, that feeling to want something. To feel like she had a purpose.' (p.245)

August and her older sister Jedda initially live in a town called Sunshine, five hours from Massacre Plains, with young parents whom August thinks of as 'rookies' (p.39). Her mother, Jolene, drinks heavily and uses other drugs, and would 'snuggle with them when she was high and play with them when she was drunk' (p.38). After her parents are arrested, the girls live with their grandparents, Albert and Elsie, at Prosperous House. August lives there until she is in high school when, after her cousin Joey is arrested and jailed for a petty crime that August and her friend Eddie also participated in, she leaves town and travels across the country. She supports herself by doing itinerant work such as fruit picking, before eventually moving to England. She only returns from England when she hears that her grandfather has died.

August struggles to deal with the trauma of her childhood: the arrest of her parents for growing marijuana when she was eight, the sexual abuse she and her sister suffered at the hands of their Uncle Jimmy, and Jedda's disappearance. As a result, she finds herself in a state of suspense, unable to move forward with her life and managing an eating disorder:

> Hadn't she done nothing all these years? Hadn't she just washed dishes, like when they were kids doing the chores at home? Hadn't she not eaten properly forever? Hadn't she wasted herself to stay a girl forever, *little girls forever*? (p.164)

August's character is marked by a seeking for something that will help her life make sense, and it is only after a decade away that she realises the answers are actually at home, on her ancestral land.

Eddie Falstaff

Key quote

'Eddie had stood out in Massacre more than a Gondiwindi even. He had always been tall and protected in a frame like that.' (p.57)

Eddie Falstaff is the son of the primary settler family in Massacre Plains, the Falstaffs of Southerly House. Even during the drought his family is one of the wealthiest and most prominent in the area. Eddie is close friends with August, despite the barriers that his mother puts in place: for example, August remembers when neither she nor Louise Hong, whose family owns the local Chinese restaurant, were invited to Eddie's birthday party, because it would make others 'uncomfortable' (p.58).

Eddie has always been in love with August, but when she turns him down he is capable of great cruelty, angrily deriding her culture and telling her that his father has been donating Gondiwindi artefacts to the city museum as the 'Falstaff Collection' for many years.

Eddie is, in many ways, the counterpoint to August. They have a great deal in common, but are ultimately widely divergent in perspective. August is raised by her grandfather, who is deeply connected to the land, and her grandmother, a city girl who comes to live in the country. Eddie, in contrast, is raised by his parents, a father who is born to the land and a mother who hates the country (p.211). August has experienced the childhood trauma of her parents' arrest, and Eddie has experienced his parents' separation (p.212). But whereas August feels connected to her Country, Eddie feels trapped: their association with the land manifests differently for each of them, and Eddie ultimately settles in the city, where he enrols in a university and begins a family (p.306).

The novel does not encourage the reader to see Eddie as a villain, but, as with Rev. Greenleaf, is explicit about the ways in which his privileged position makes him at times arrogant and even cruel.

Elsie Gondiwindi (Nana)

Key quotes

'After I met my beautiful wife, although beauty was the least of her, strong and fearless was the most of her – well she taught me lots of things.' (p.2)

'Elsie opened her mouth and a deep noise came out, words she didn't remember that she'd gathered like years.' (p.162)

Unlike Albert, who is born and raised on Country, Elsie teaches at a university in the city (most likely Sydney University, from which the Freedom Ride was organised), and meets Albert when she is part of the Freedom Ride in 1965 (p.281). She is much more a city person than a country girl, as Albert's anecdote about the koala demonstrates, but she becomes a core part of life at Massacre Plains and a significant figure in the Gondiwindi family. Albert's death is a devastating blow to her, especially as it is coupled with the need to leave Prosperous House to make way for the mine. The news about Jedda at the end of the novel is a further blow, although Jedda has been missing for many years.

Elsie has always been committed to civil rights, and not only in the Freedom Ride. When Joey and August join the anti-mine protestors, Elsie declares: 'without protest, we wouldn't have our rights, none of us would have civil rights, the vote, decent working week' (p.299). Elsie says, 'We're just the world's quarry of choice and I don't see any way around that' (p.299), echoing the view of Albert's mother, Augustine, that 'the Aborigine is a pity' (p.11). However, Elsie's reaction is to be active and to fight. She tells August that one of the reasons she loved Albert was because 'we were both Koori ... we would lift each other because we both knew we needed it' (p.116). This echoes Albert's comment that Elsie 'taught me I wasn't just a second-rate man raised on white flour and Christianity' (p.2). After Albert's death, August thinks that Elsie looks 'aged, as if gone to seed' (p.19). However, by the end of the novel Elsie is buttressed by the support of her family, including August's return and Jolene's release from jail, and the relief of finally knowing what happened to Jedda.

Reverend Ferdinand Greenleaf

Key quotes

'If I had known then what great burden would befall me, would later exhaust me, then I think I wouldn't have rested on my knees that night at all.' (pp.74–5)

'I fear my truth will go unnoticed and my life will simply be reduced to the coat of arms of a distant land.' (p.269)

A Lutheran minister of German heritage, Ferdinand Greenleaf arrives in South Australia with his family in the mid-nineteenth century and is raised in the largely German community there.

He spends thirty-four years (p.50) as the missionary in charge of the Prosperous Mission at Massacre Plains, which he founds in 1880. During this period, he becomes increasingly appalled by the brutality with which Aboriginal people are treated and the refusal of the colonial authorities to do anything about the massacres and widespread sexual violence. Despised by the people of the nearby town for his role at the Mission and his attempts to bring violent offenders to the attention of the law, he is interned, along with other men of German heritage, at the beginning of World War I – at this time, authorities feared that German Australians might be spies or else would return to Germany and fight against the Allies. He is held first at Torrens Island in South Australia (a cyclical return to the place where he first lived in Australia) and then at Holsworthy Internment Camp near Sydney, where he dies. In his captivity, he writes a long letter to a member of the British Society of Ethnography, setting out the history of the Mission and the violence that he witnessed and was subjected to. This letter forms part of Albert Gondiwindi's Native Title application.

Jedda Gondiwindi

Key quotes

'In her mind ten-year-old Jedda is backlit, running from the attic room, down the stairs, leaping off the verandah and through the fields before the cutting.' (p.22)

'And just like that the home became just a house, they never really talked about Jedda Gondiwindi again.' (p.27)

Jedda Gondiwindi is a minor character in that she disappears long before the novel's beginning and is only present in others' memories of her. But she is a major character in terms of her effect on the narrative. Her disappearance is a key factor in August's eating disorder, her sense of isolation and disconnectedness, and her separation from her home and country (in both senses of the word). Additionally, Jedda's disappearance is one of the core mysteries whose answer is revealed in Albert's dictionary.

The elder of the two Gondiwindi sisters by twelve months, Jedda lives, like August, for the first few years of her life in Sunshine, some five hours away from Massacre Plains. Because her mother, Jolene, is often either drunk or on drugs, Jedda takes on a motherly role with August. August remembers how they would cook dinner together while their mother slept and 'when she woke up they'd have washed their plates, brushed their teeth, and they would be tucked in, Jedda tucked August first and then herself' (p.39). This motherliness plays a key role in Jedda's death, as August remembers that 'Jedda led Uncle Jimmy Corvette away from August. Jedda saved her' (p.166).

Even as a child, Jedda is fascinated by dance, even in the middle of karate class: 'She never could stay still, she was always dancing how she liked, moving to music no-one else could hear' (p.55). Both Albert and August believe that Jedda lives on in the brolga – Albert because his ancestors have told him so and August because she recognises her long-limbed, dancing sister in the brolga that comes and dances at Albert's funeral.

Joey Gondiwindi

Key quote

'Joey had known some things when they were kids, known before the other kids did that adults lie, that they can be mean and bad. […] He heard something in the world the way she [August] smelt and tasted it.' (pp.143–4)

Joey Gondiwindi is August's cousin, the son of Aunt Missy and the only grandson of Albert and Elsie. His sister, Rosie, is significantly younger, only ten at the time of Albert's death (p.144). He is fond and protective of his mother (he does not wish her to be hurt during the protest, for example), but estranged from his father (p.145). Joey is optimistic where August can be fatalistic, but he is also much more knowledgeable, earlier than his cousins, of the risks and dangers in the world, especially to young Aboriginal people (pp.143–4).

Joey is a friend and companion of August in her teenage years. He is with August and Eddie when the pharmacy catches fire (p.86), but Joey, who is keeping watch, is the only one who is caught (p.287). Only fourteen at the time, he is tried as a juvenile (unlike his cousins, who have been tried as adults for other crimes), but he does spend the final year of his four-year sentence in an adult prison, after he turns seventeen (p.141). His arrest is the last straw for August, who skips school to attend his trial and then, when he is jailed, goes home, packs and leaves for a series of itinerant jobs, not returning to Prosperous House for ten years.

Joey tells August that in prison he receives the equivalent of three university degrees, because reading is the only thing to do (p.142). He focuses on two topics. The most prominent one is computer programming; Missy is particularly proud of his development of an app called *Get 'Em*: 'It's this game where you fight the colonisers – you can pick your weapons and which country you want to fight for and everything' (p.64). But he also reads about Native Title, especially the work done by Eddie Koiki Mabo, and speaks extensively with Albert about claiming Native Title on the Prosperous House land (pp.142–3).

Aunt Missy

Key quote

> 'Albert wasn't finished but Missy dismissed him – she was sick to the guts, sick in that place.' (p.263)

One of Albert and Elsie's three daughters, along with Nicki and Jolene, Missy is the mother of Joey and Rosie. She is proud of the ways in which her son has survived his prison sentence and used his time there so productively (p.64). She is protective of her mother, as indicated by her reaction when the Rinepalm official turns up at Elsie's house (p.238). Like her father, she is strongly connected to the land, and has also looked for ways to claim Native Title, although she has been blocked by the fact that the artefacts are stored at the museum under the name 'Falstaff' (p.232). Like her mother, she is not afraid to speak up when she feels the situation is unfair. She joins the protest against the mine, chaining herself to the fence alongside August and Joey (p.296), and also challenges the museum security guard, who tries to prevent August from taking photographs (p.261). She is, perhaps, the one of the three daughters who is most like her parents: closer to Prosperous House than Nicki and without Jolene's issues with drugs and alcohol.

Aunt Nicki

Key quote

> 'And Aunt Nicki … with eyes closed, asked the Lord, whom she never asked for anything, to end this chapter of their lives.' (p.162)

Of the three daughters of Albert and Elsie, Nicki is the one most removed from Prosperous House and most embedded in colonial power structures. She works for the local council and lives in the 'nice part of town' called the 'Minties area' (p.277), which is 'where the middle class lived, according to a census like theirs' (p.14). Nicki is elegant and self-possessed, although her response when August drops in unannounced at the council chambers suggests that she keeps her family and working life separate (p.186).

Nicki takes and conceals Albert's dictionary, both the manuscript and the cassette recordings of Albert trying to remember how to pronounce the words, as well as the Native Title application he had been preparing. Her reasons for doing this are never entirely clear. August thinks at first that she might have been bribed by the mining company (p.278), but later seems to rethink this (p.289). She could be protecting Aunt Mary from the truth about her son (Jimmy Corvette) or about his death, or she could be protecting Elsie from knowing that Jedda is gone forever. August also wonders whether Nicki was also molested as a child (p.306). Her sense of separation from the family is confirmed when 'much later Aunt Nicki moved to the city' (p.306), as Eddie does.

Great Aunt Mary

Key quote

'What a thing it was for us children without parents around to be hugged. I think my sister Mary never got a hug at the Girls' Home because in a warm embrace she froze.' (p.42)

Albert's younger sister, Mary is born after the family arrives at the Mission; later she is separated from her mother and sent to a children's home. Mary has one child, Jimmy, who she loves but whose true nature she cannot see: August reflects that Mary 'didn't know about the bad in her own son' (p.60). At Albert's funeral, Mary thinks about 'when she buried her own son, how much she'd loved him, more than she knew she could, more than she was ever taught' (p.162). Mary's love for Jimmy is rooted in the trauma of her separation from her own family. It is possible that Aunt Nicki suppresses Albert's manuscript because it reveals that Jimmy sexually abused both August and Jedda, killed Jedda, and was himself killed by Albert.

After being separated when the Mission is turned into a station following the arrest of Rev. Greenleaf, the siblings meet again almost by chance at the Aboriginal Medical Centre in Massacre, during a Christmas lunch: 'they didn't know whether to hug or dance in the joy' (p.162). Mary is taken in by Albert and Elsie when Jimmy is young, although both Albert and Elsie have doubts about Jimmy, who 'harboured secrets and nursed great contempt for people wherever he went', while his mother is 'nothing but good and hardworking' (p.79). Later, Mary lives in the part of town called Vegemite Valley, 'where her door remained open for the priest always' (p.85).

THEMES, IDEAS & VALUES

Colonialism

Key quotes

'I remember walking out onto the landing of the Boys' Home, standing under the sign that used to hang outside – Think White. Act White. Be White.' (p.23)

'There was a war here against the local people. In that war the biggest victim was the culture, you know?' (p.92)

'Don't know what it is about us that seems to rile the white man. The burden, the burden of their memory perhaps, or that we weren't extinguished with the lights of those empires after all.' (p.160)

The consequences of colonisation are central to *The Yield*, from the placenames and the language to the characters' experiences. Although the initial process of colonising Massacre Plains happened long before the events of the main narrative, Winch does not treat colonisation as a past event, but as one that is continually resonating through to the current generations. For example, consider this vivid image from near the end of the novel:

> a digger felled the last peppercorn tree and white things tumbled from the dirt and roots, like sticks of quartz, like bones. A waterfall of yellowed bones. [...] The cemetery was found in the more productive area of the property, and the remains in the paddock had been mistakenly ploughed and cropped by the Falstaffs. (p.305)

This land, which is so important to the Gondiwindis and so central to the lives of the Falstaffs, is quite literally a graveyard.

Furthermore, the multi-voiced narrative in *The Yield* serves to emphasise the ongoing nature of colonisation and the traumas that it can continue to cause for colonised peoples. The narratives include Albert's dictionary, which exists in a temporally undefined space of the present and the past together; Rev. Greenleaf's letter, which recounts events beginning roughly a century after the First Fleet landed (the Mission is founded in 1880); and the much more contemporary narrative focused on August. In each of these, colonisation makes its mark on the people and the landscape.

Albert's ancestors, for example, talk about the effect of smallpox, the scars of which Albert can see on the bodies of the ancestors who visit him (p.45). Later, they attempt to point out the less visible scars that mark the former presence of houses on the land, with wooden walls and clay roofs returned to the soil (p.203). These are physical markers of the consequences of colonisation; they are scars of something brought (diseases) and scars of something taken away (homes). Rev. Greenleaf's narrative also describes physical scars, such as those on Daisy after she is attacked by local white men (p.122), on the body of Wowhely when he is murdered (p.173) and on the boys brutally whipped by a Station master (pp.196–7).

But the Mission also leaves less visible scars; for example, those caused by the separation of families, which Rev. Greenleaf, despite his sympathetic stance, facilitates (p.122). In the present, Albert talks about the ways in which Prosperous House is a beacon for people who were raised there in the days of the Mission, 'returning to make peace' (p.157). When he speaks to Missy in the museum, Albert also emphasises the hidden and secret ways of dividing and destroying colonised people: 'They gave us blankets, Missy – they took the land that way, too – with smallpox-infected blankets! They put arsenic in the flour, Missy!' (pp.262–3). The narrative about August also reveals ongoing trauma, often invisible. She thinks, as she drives through Vegemite Valley, of the 'broken homes, where shame-filled single mothers brought up silent boys who became angry later in life', as opposed to the 'doorbells and locked gates' where the Minties live (p.14).

Key point

One of the strengths of *The Yield* is its complex narrative structure, in which the three narrative threads intersect and resonate with each other. As a modern Aboriginal woman, August's perspective is a contemporary one as she looks at historical artefacts and reads Rev. Greenleaf's narrative, the physical markers of the past that carry into the present. Rev. Greenleaf's letter is contemporary to him, but historical to the reader and August; and Albert's dictionary, particularly when he describes his encounters with his ancestors, has a sense of timelessness. Through these intersecting narratives, Winch emphasises that colonialism is simultaneously something that has happened, is happening and will happen.

> Colonisation is a complex event that has affected different colonised people in different ways. Although people have used the term 'postcolonial' to describe countries colonised by Great Britain and other European powers, critics are increasingly drawing out the ways in which colonial practices and their consequences are still affecting people today. The discussion of colonialism in this section of the guide is only a starting place for thinking about colonialism in *The Yield*: the reference section at the end of this guide includes suggestions for further reading.

Language and literacy

Key quotes

'All the words I found on the wind.' (p.3)

'She realised she'd fled there for Jedda, but that she had stayed there looking for those words that she'd understand, that would explain what it all meant.' (p.308)

'Maybe you are looking for a statue, or a bench by the banks of the Murrumby to honour the people who lived by the river. Better, there is water returning, nudging what was dead. Better the *burral-gang* congregate here often. Better these words and better we are still here and that we speak them.' (p.310)

When Aboriginal people were removed from Country to stations, missions and children's homes, they were forbidden to speak their own language and required to speak English. As Aunt Nicki says to August, 'They grew up on the Mish, remember, and language wasn't allowed' (p.146), where 'language' specifically means Wiradjuri language. Speaking of it in such absolute terms, as 'language' rather than 'Wiradjuri' or 'Wiradjuri language', reinforces its centrality to daily life and culture: it is so central that the speaker does not need to clarify which language is being referred to. When people are forbidden to speak their language, the very act of not speaking it becomes a tool for further disenfranchisement: 'Our people's language is extinct, no-one speaks it any more so they [the mine] can tick that box on their government form that says "loss of cultural connection"' (p.146). In other words, the language is forbidden, so people do not speak it; because it is not spoken, authorities can claim that it has been lost.

Wiradjuri language has been subject to particularly strong language rebuilding. Sometimes called 'language revival' or 'language reclamation', language rebuilding in Australia focuses on the revitalisation of Aboriginal languages. In Wiradjuri Country, this has been the focus of work by, among others, Wiradjuri Elder Stan Grant Senior and his collaborator John Rudder, who have been producing books, especially for children, in Wiradjuri for many years, and compiled *A New Wiradjuri Dictionary* (2010). Both Stan Grant Senior and John Rudder are instrumental to Albert Gondiwindi's dictionary, as is the Parkes Wiradjuri Language Group, who helped establish initiatives such as teaching Wiradjuri in Parkes primary schools (for more detail, see Winch's Acknowledgements on page 343). More information on language is given in the 'Genre, structure & language' section of this guide.

Beyond this emphasis on language, however, is a broader emphasis on literacy. Albert's literacy is of great value to him in a variety of ways, and he credits Elsie with teaching him to write as well as read (p.2). For Albert, writing is a way of sharing culture and knowledge. He notes that he and his people have, historically, been written *about*:

> just like the Reverend once wrote the births and baptisms at the Mission, like the station manager wrote rations at the Station and just like the ma'ams and masters wrote our good behaviour at the Boys' Home ... (p.2)

This is writing as codifying and as controlling. But Albert places more emphasis on recording: 'I am writing because the spirits are urging me to remember, and because the town needs to know that I remember' (p.2). This concept is foundational in the novel.

Similarly, Joey's time in juvenile detention and then prison (from fourteen to eighteen) is a period in which, he tells August, there was 'nothing to do there but read' (p.142). One outcome is his computer app, *Get 'Em*: 'this game where you fight the colonisers' (p.64). Like Albert's dictionary, this is another form of storytelling and of taking control of a narrative that might otherwise be used to codify or control. It is not only Joey who takes control of the narrative; the game allows the players to take control themselves, to 'pick your weapons and which country you want to fight for and everything' (p.64). Joey also reads about Native Title, and discusses the possibilities with Albert, so that his literacy, like Albert's, leads him back to the ancestors' stories.

Books are important to August, something she sees as a connection with her grandfather: 'She loved her books, the pages filled with company when she was all alone, having those few moveable possessions that were often lost, waterlogged or never returned yet had a way of replacing themselves' (p.62). The authors listed throughout the novel include British fantasy writers (JRR Tolkien, CS Lewis, Roald Dahl), classic authors (Jane Austen, Charles Dickens, WB Yeats, Omar Khayyam, Rūmī), modern authors (William Faulkner, Sylvia Plath, Jorge Luis Borges), and authors of mainstream children's literature (Ann M Martin's *Baby-Sitters Club*, RL Stine's *Goosebumps*). But August also finds that reading can be alienating, since 'in every mobile-library book, she could never find herself or her sister' (p.62). This sense of representation is not all she looks for in books, but it is something that she cannot find.

Racism

Key quotes

'Years later, even after those laws about the public pools and the cinema seating changed, I could still recognise that fear that people had towards us, that distrust they had of our kids, and since that day I saw Elsie at the *galing* I've been reminded time and time again that people's attitudes don't change just because the law changes.' (p. 283)

'The man turned back again. "You like that?" he asked her, pointing to it, without waiting for an answer. "That's the Southern Cross, lady. That means you don't belong here."' (p.237)

'What have I done, dear Dr Cross, that I feel such guilt in replacing *Baymee* with the Lord? What right had I to erasure? What right did I have to say one belief begets another?' (pp.270–1)

Racism is central to *The Yield,* which is, in part, a novel about the long-term, far-reaching traumas experienced by people when one culture violently and persistently represses and marginalises another. We see the historical presence of racism in Rev. Greenleaf's letter, which recounts rapes, attacks on the Mission and the abuse of Aboriginal women through violence and alcohol. Greenleaf's account also highlights the judiciary's lack of concern about white violence towards Aboriginal people: he notes that few cases ever came before the courts and 'all cases of this nature were indulged in by the judges turning their heads or at most imposing the cost of a paltry fine' (p.197).

However, although Greenleaf is a sympathetic man who wishes to do good in the world, the Mission is also born of a belief in white superiority, and of the need to impose Western cultural mores (including Christian beliefs and practices) on Aboriginal people. Although Greenleaf learns about local farming and fishing practices (p.151) and 'gathered with the men and gave sermons about *Him*, neither the Lord nor *Baymee*' (p.152), these actions occur under the overarching aegis (guidance) of the Lutheran Church. Furthermore, his approach is paternalistic (like that of an overprotective father) and constitutes another form of racism: although couched as concern for welfare, it is patronising in its assumptions that Aboriginal people are childlike, incapable of caring for themselves and requiring the oversight of missions, stations and children's homes. The justification of the removal of children from their parents is couched in very similar terms.

The paternalistic approach of Greenleaf and other missionaries has long-term consequences, as we can see in the Gondiwindi family. It costs them their language and, with their language, parts of their culture, which Albert painstakingly begins to restore with the help of his ancestors. It also fractures family ties. Albert later reconnects with his mother and sister, but his mother succumbs to alcoholism: 'she let herself do the most insulting thing she could think of – take the poison they brought with them and go to town' (p.11). Albert's sister Mary, meanwhile, raised almost from birth in a girls' home, struggles with emotional expression and affection (p.26), and her own son abuses the younger members of the family. In the homes, the children are 'ranked' by their skin colour, as Albert indicates when he describes the sesquicentenary performances: 'We had to act like gentry, the octoroon boys the most, the full-blood boys not at all' (p.77). Everything is structured around the concept of *deficit*.

Key point

The *deficit model* (or *cultural deficit model*) is a longstanding approach to modelling cultural difference, not only in Australia but also in countries such as the United States. As the name suggests, it is based on the idea that what differentiates a minority culture from the majority is what it lacks (the deficit). This model has been influential for many years, but its negative framing is problematic in a number of ways. Recently, the focus has shifted to the more positive *cultural difference model*, which, like its predecessor, recognises difference but, unlike the deficit model, frames this in a positive, enriching and supportive way.

In *The Yield*, the white people involved in running the missions and the children's homes never emphasise the positive elements of Aboriginal culture and identity (although Rev. Greenleaf takes some steps towards this), but rather only talk negatively about what the children are *not* – that is, how they fail to measure against the artificially imposed standards of white colonial society.

Albert's dictionary – like *The Yield* itself – is a means of working against this idea of deficit, of reclaiming, emphasising and sharing the positive, nurturing aspects of Aboriginal culture, as he remembers them from before he was sent to a boys' home, as he learns them from his ancestors and as he rediscovers them 'on the wind' (p.3).

Family

Key quotes

'"The family trees of people like us are just bushes now, aren't they?" he said. "Someone has been trimming them good." I wouldn't ever forget these words because they sounded like sad poems. And I guess that's a true thing, because all the years I've lived I've lost so many parts of the people that make me up.' (p.25)

'She thought about how every family has its own special language. Its own weird sense of humour that's stuck in the past.' (p.138)

'She and Joey learnt it's the grandkids who inherit everything their ancestors did before. They carried the past with them, though they never knew.' (p.308)

One of the happy elements at the ending of *The Yield* is the fact that:

> August is still there in Massacre Plains, in the Valley with her nana and Aunt Missy and Aunt Mary too. All the family, all the Gondiwindi mob. All the women together, Joey too. (p.308)

The novel is a story of homecoming, of August being able to reconcile with a family that was first damaged by removals (Albert's removal from his mother and sister; August and Jedda's removal from their parents), disappearances (Jedda's) and deaths (Uncle Jimmy's and Albert's), and then further damaged by August's long separation (voluntary, but driven by trauma, guilt and grief) from the day-to-day family life that builds up connections, memories and relationships.

Family is of central importance to *The Yield*. Albert begins by explaining who his parents are, then introduces himself and his wife. He explores this in his dictionary, in *dhaganhu ngurambang* ('Where is your country?'):

> The question is not really about a place on the map. When our people say *Where is your country* they are asking something deeper. *Who is your family? Who are you related to? Are we related?* (pp.33–4)

As well as finding words on the wind, he is also gathering family members – both good and bad – who have been scattered, in the stories contained in his dictionary. Albert's funeral becomes a large, family-centred celebration of life, bringing August back into the centre of Prosperous House and enabling her to reconcile with her cousin.

Family is not, however, always a positive structure. The Gondiwindis are a large and loving family, despite their occasional quarrelsomeness. Indeed, as August suggests, this quarrelsomeness might even be part of what ties the family together: 'The Gondiwindi sense of humour, she knew, was bickering until laughter' (p.138). Eddie's family at Southerly House, however, hides its own fracture lines. Eddie's family is rural royalty; August reflects that 'Eddie Falstaff didn't need to lie about the contents of his home – even during the drought, he was almost the richest kid in all of Massacre Plains' (p.58). The house, with its ever-changing exterior paint, diamond-patterned paths and smooth swathe of grass, fascinates August. But the family relationships within it are fractured. Eddie notes that his mother hated farm life and living in the country (p.211). August remembers, too, when Eddie's father was found to have been visiting 'a massage therapist in Broken' and 'Eddie's mum beat Eddie's dad with a fresh strip of willow branch as he left the property' (p.212). Eddie's mother also puts barriers in the way of Eddie's friendships with August and Louise Hong: 'Eddie thought his mother was talking about girl-germs, but August knew it was something else' (p.58). With all this resentment behind the walls of Southerly House, it is unsurprising that Eddie feels trapped by his family and by the land that is his family's inheritance (p.217).

These are the two most defined examples of family in the text, but there are also single-parent families, including Great Aunt Mary and her son, Uncle Jimmy Corvette, and Aunt Missy and her children Joey and Rosie. While Mary's son turns out badly, the novel does not connect this to her single-parent status. Missy's children, unlike Jimmy, are warmly connected to the family, affectionate and considerate of their mother. Note, for example, Joey's insistence that his mother step away from the protest when it becomes violent (p.300).

Trauma

Key quotes

'August was reminded of when Jedda disappeared for too long, how the family had drawn inside, their sadness like a still life.' (p.19)

'August thought she looked less spry and even more grey in the head than she'd been before. She was still tall, but everyone was – everyone still had their height.' (p.60)

'See, pain travels through our family tree like a songline. We've been singing our pain into a solid thing. The old ones, the young ones too, are ready to heal.' (p.312)

Trauma manifests in *The Yield* in a number of ways: the discussion of colonialism above is also an examination of trauma. This section focuses on more personal, individual trauma, while recognising that this can be exacerbated by broader traumas that affect communities and cultures. For example, August carries within her two traumas, one that is apparent from early in the novel and one that emerges later: the disappearance of her sister when August was nine, and the arrest and jailing of her cousin Joey when August was a teenager. Jedda's disappearance is traumatic for the whole Gondiwindi family. For August, who had lost her mother and father to prison a year earlier (and her father to death not long after that), the trauma completely reshapes her, both physically (through her compulsion to starve herself, to keep herself small, thin and childlike as she was when Jedda disappeared) and psychologically (leading her to distance herself from her family and home, and to move to England, a decision influenced by Jedda's fascination with that country).

The circumstances leading to the jailing of Joey are only gradually revealed. The reader knows early on that Joey has recently been released from prison and that, now he has been released, he is making use of the computer skills he learnt while in juvenile detention (p.64). August later reflects that 'only Joey had been caught' when the pharmacy caught fire, although August and Eddie were both there (p.86). When August and Joey reunite at Albert's funeral, the reader learns that August ran away from home the day Joey was sentenced (p.141). Only near the end of the novel does the reader learn that Joey was caught because Eddie told him to keep watch, and that he feels he was abandoned by his cousin and her friend, who saved themselves from prison (p.287). This slow revelation of the trauma in this family relationship mimics the slow work of recognising and addressing trauma, a process that takes time and effort. Similarly, although the truth about Jedda's disappearance is revealed to the family at the end of the novel, the trauma it caused is not easily addressed. August indicates this when she speculates about Aunt Nicki: 'perhaps someone had hurt her when she was a little girl, too. Or maybe she was protecting Aunt Mary. No-one really understood, not yet' (p.306). The novel ends with this process still in play: no one really understands yet, and perhaps they will never entirely understand.

The Yield itself is also a process of writing out and understanding trauma, though on a broader, national level. The novel is unflinching about the violence perpetrated at the Mission and in the surrounding country: both the physical violence committed by the townspeople, and also the less visible trauma created by the loss of family, culture and language. The character for whom this is most apparent, perhaps, is Augustine, Albert's mother, who was born at the Prosperous Mission. Albert says that his mother 'died an old woman by the grip of, well, it was an Old World disease too' (p.1). This reference to Augustine's death from alcoholism is at the beginning of the novel, and Albert's separation from his mother as well as his longing to find her during his time travels (e.g. p.78, p.159) permeate the novel. The resulting trauma is one that, perhaps, no one entirely understands, but, like the trauma of Jedda's disappearance written down in Albert's dictionary, the process of writing it out helps the process of understanding.

Key point

One recurring idea in *The Yield* is that of *animism*: the belief that plants, inanimate objects and natural phenomena have living souls. (Like most spiritual beliefs, animism has much more complexity to it than a simple definition can indicate.) Animism is central to Albert's perspective (and shared by Missy), and he refers to it throughout his dictionary. It also links some of the themes discussed in this guide. If place, for example, has a living soul, then trauma can be visited on it as well as on people. Similarly, colonialism affects not only people, but also the plants (loss of native vegetation) and land (ploughed over and planted), which share living souls with the people who live on and with them.

DIFFERENT INTERPRETATIONS

Different interpretations arise from different responses to a text. Over time, a text will evoke a wide range of responses from its readers, who may come from various social or cultural groups and live in very different places and historical periods. Responses by critics and reviewers can be published in newspapers, journals and books, both online and in print. They can also be expressed in discussions among readers in the media, classrooms, book groups and so on.

While there is no single correct reading or interpretation of a text, it is important to understand that an interpretation is more than a personal opinion – it is the justification of a point of view on the text. To present an interpretation of a text based on your point of view, you must use a logical argument and support it with relevant evidence from the text.

Critical viewpoints

Aboriginal Australians have been the subject of extensive anthropological, linguistic and ethnographic studies, in part because Aboriginal cultures are the oldest continuous living cultures on earth. However, it is important to make a distinction between works that are written *about* and works that are written *by*, especially when you are examining a colonised community. The reference section of this guide includes works by First Nations writers on topics such as Aboriginal agriculture, the colonial treatment of Aboriginal women, and Wiradjuri culture and history.

At the time of writing there is not a large body of criticism specifically about *The Yield*. Winch's earlier works, however, have been subject to a range of critical interpretations, particularly her first, highly successful collection, *Swallow the Air*. This section looks at critical viewpoints on *The Yield* as well as on Winch's earlier works.

Speaking broadly about Winch's writing, Paul Sharrad emphasises that she sits at an intersection of national and international contexts, as an author who has enjoyed wide success in Australia but has also been based outside Australia for many years. This has been a common line of enquiry for critics of Australian writing: the question of the extent to which Australian fiction is primarily national or whether it appeals just as much to international readers (this is sometimes called the 'transnational turn'). For Aboriginal writing, this can be, as Sharrad sets out, a particularly important question, especially when we come to think of Australia not as 'a' country, but as a number of (Aboriginal) Countries within a continent. Novels by writers such as Kim Scott (Noongar), Alexis Wright (Waanyi) and Melissa Lucashenko (Bundjalung) are strongly connected to a particular Country.

The Yield is tied closely to Wiradjuri Country, but it also speaks to common experiences of colonialism across different Aboriginal Countries, so it can be regarded as 'transnational' within Australia, or, to use Sharrad's term for Winch's *Swallow the Air*, 'trans(intra)national' (Sharrad 2020, p.6). Further, in winning national prizes, especially the prestigious Miles Franklin Literary Award, and being translated and published in countries outside Australia, it is also 'transnational' globally. Indeed, Sharrad points out that *The Yield* is Winch's first international publication (p.10). Sharrad notes that '*Swallow the Air* does rest on a claim on selfhood as belonging to a country, family and language group, and its ending suggests an assertion of belonging to a nation-wide community of Indigenous Australians' (p.6). This is also true of *The Yield*, although Sharrad suggests that this novel, with its three very different but connected narratives, 'also shows how the elements of transnational across, through and beyond do not add up seamlessly to a tidy sum that can be slipped into any comfortably homogenous nation narrative' (Sharrad 2020, p.11).

Sue Kossew also talks about Winch as a transnational author whose work, connecting the local and the global, reminds 'readers of the ongoing global after-effects of colonisation, and the ways in which violence and survival are common to both' (Kossew 2019, p.178). But her focus is more on the ways in which Winch's work (especially her second collection, *After the Carnage*) explores the ideas of precarity and survival, which are also evident in *The Yield*. 'Precarity' is a state of uncertainty and marginalisation; it might relate to uncertain or unsteady employment and poverty. August's parents, for example, are both labelled as 'unemployed' on her birth certificate. But *The Yield* also explores the precarity of home. Prosperous House is precarious for a few reasons: because the Falstaffs did not pay off the freehold and the land became crown land; because the drought has rendered the town desperate for a means of survival besides farming; and because it sits on a large tin deposit. Prosperous House is also precarious as a home for August because the disappearances of Jedda and – later – Uncle Jimmy make it unsafe and insecure. This precarity is also written large on Country as a whole, where the long stewardship of the Wiradjuri people is made precarious by colonialism, the removal of people and the suppression of culture. 'Precarity' is a way of thinking through 'Indigenous Australians still coping with the intergenerational trauma of colonial dispossession and of family disintegration as the result of government policies' (Kossew 2019, p.180).

More recently, Palawa scholar Alice Bellette has analysed *The Yield* as an example of Aboriginal Gothic. Gothic fiction emerged in England in the mid-eighteenth century, and continued to be popular throughout the nineteenth century and into the twentieth and twenty-first centuries. Key examples include nineteenth-century novels such as Bram Stoker's *Dracula*, twentieth-century novels such as Daphne du Maurier's *Rebecca* and Anne Rice's *Interview with the Vampire*, and contemporary television series such as *Penny Dreadful*. The core elements of the Gothic include the return of repressed, concealed or unspoken things; hidden and monstrous aspects of human nature; the idea of the uncanny, or a strangeness in otherwise familiar things; and a fascination with the societies and cultures of the past.

Although the Gothic is originally European in focus (its name comes from the architecture of the European Middle Ages), Bellette argues that 'while Aboriginal writing is not obligated to respond to colonial writing, writing into traditions with our own perspectives has the power to destabilise and unsettle dominant narratives that were constructed without our consent' (Bellette 2022, p.256). That is, 'Aboriginal authors are using the tropes [concepts] that populate European gothic fiction for political ends to demonstrate resistance to colonisation' (p.256). Some of the aspects of *The Yield* that draw on the Gothic tradition include the revelation of family secrets, embedded manuscripts, multiple narratives, the strangeness of the familiar (particularly through August's perspective) and the hidden monstrousness in human nature. Bellette also points to a 'colonial obsession with blood' (p.260), literally and in terms of heritage, which is evident in *The Yield* in Albert's memories of the sesquicentenary (p.77) and Aunt Missy's suggestion that they should have 'a museum of tanks of blood' (p.262). Returning to the idea of transnational Aboriginal literature, Bellette acknowledges the European focus of the Gothic, but emphasises that novels such as *The Yield* can 'repurpose and reimagine' some of its tropes in a 'powerful mode of resisting by literary means' (Bellette 2022, p.264).

Two interpretations

Reading 1: *The Yield* is essentially optimistic.

The Yield contains some deeply traumatic moments and events, but ultimately it is an optimistic novel. Although it does not conclude with a simple or easy happy ending, it does offer hope and healing in its final pages.

The novel describes or refers to traumatic experiences that have occurred in both the distant and the relatively recent past. The most explicit of these, perhaps, are the massacres and incidents of sexual violence occurring around the Mission, the sexual violence experienced by August and Jedda as children, the disappearance of Jedda and the murder of Uncle Jimmy Corvette. Each of these events is shown to have long-term consequences for the people who experienced them, and also for the people around them. Take, for example, the disappearance of Jedda. Because Jedda is never found and because the only people who know the truth choose not to reveal it, the family experiences ongoing trauma. Elsie slowly extends her garden, looking for Jedda; August runs away from home and starves herself, trying not to outgrow her forever-young sister; even Albert stops fishing for pleasure and starts fishing as an excuse to look for Jedda. The trauma is not a one-time event, but something ongoing and poisonous.

As such, the novel does not offer a straightforward happy ending. Even when the truth of Jedda's disappearance is revealed to the family, the trauma that it has caused cannot be immediately undone. August, for example, needs time to heal both psychologically and, because she has been starving herself, physically. Furthermore, the discovery itself is a traumatic event: although family members now know what happened to Jedda, they also have to come to terms with the revelations about Uncle Jimmy. Great Aunt Mary, in particular, must accept that her son not only sexually assaulted his nieces, but murdered one of them.

Nevertheless, the novel does offer hope and healing. Although it is explicit about the fact that recovery from trauma takes time and effort, it ends with a sense that some things can and will get better. After years of drought, the novel ends with rainfall; the rain is not a magical cure, but it provides short-term relief and is a sign of hope and renewal, an indication that not even the drought will last forever, and the platypus might return to the Murrumby, as the Gondiwindis return to Prosperous House. Similarly, August's mother's release from prison is a bittersweet moment, not least because August's father did not survive his prison sentence, but it is a hopeful one, another homecoming. *The Yield* is a realistic book, but it is also an optimistic one.

Reading 2: *The Yield* is essentially pessimistic.

Although *The Yield* ends with some positive events, there are bigger issues within the novel that will take a long time to resolve, if a resolution can ever be achieved. The novel demonstrates that trauma can be carried through the generations, and it also contains traumatic events, such as an ongoing drought, that are too large and far-reaching for an easy solution.

The Yield makes it clear that trauma can persist and affect successive generations. Albert, for example, is clearly haunted by his mother's alcoholism; he is always looking for the mother he knew before they were separated, but he can never find her, even in his time travels. The novel also indicates that some of the traumatic events it recounts might be revisited. For example, there are homes in Vegemite Valley where 'shame-filled single mothers brought up silent boys who became angry later in life' (p.14). Later, August drives past Aunt Mary's home, also in Vegemite Valley, 'where she had brought up her son' (pp.84–5). The implication is that, although Uncle Jimmy Corvette, who assaulted August and Jedda when they were children, is dead, other men like him might still live in the community, perpetuating a cycle of abuse and despair.

Furthermore, some crises in the novel are not easily resolved. The town is suffering from a severe drought and experiencing high levels of unemployment and depression. The most vivid sign of this is when August notices that the real estate agency itself is for sale. Although Winch does not encourage readers to approve of Rinepalm's plans, the mine is expected to bring employment to the town and the novel suggests that most townspeople will be unhappy if the plans are delayed or abandoned. The rain that comes at the end of the novel brings hope that the drought will break, but it is not quite enough: the drought has lasted so long that even forty days and nights of rain only refill the Murrumby briefly, before the water is used for irrigation.

The Yield is a pessimistic novel; although it has moments of great sweetness and hope, it is also realistic, and it cannot quite commit to a happy ending.

QUESTIONS & ANSWERS

This section focuses on your own analytical writing on the text, and gives you strategies for producing high-quality responses in your coursework and exam essays.

Essay writing – an overview

An essay on a literary work is a formal and serious piece of writing that presents your point of view on the text, usually in response to a given topic. Your 'point of view' in an essay is your interpretation of the meaning of the text's language, structure, characters, situations and events, supported by detailed analysis of textual evidence.

Analyse – don't summarise

In your essays it is important to avoid simply summarising what happens in a text.

- A **summary** is a description or paraphrase (retelling in different words) of the characters and events. For example: 'Macbeth has a horrifying vision of a dagger dripping with blood before he goes to murder King Duncan.'
- An **analysis** is an explanation of the real meaning or significance that lies 'beneath' the text's words (and images, for a film). For example: 'Macbeth's vision of a bloody dagger shows how deeply uneasy he is about the violent act he is contemplating, and conveys his sense that supernatural forces are impelling him to act.'

A limited amount of summary is sometimes necessary to let your reader know which part of the text you wish to discuss. However, always keep this to a minimum and follow it immediately with your analysis of what this part of the text is really telling us.

Plan your essay

Carefully plan your essay so that you have a clear idea of what you are going to say. The plan ensures that your ideas flow logically, that your argument remains consistent and that you stay on the topic. An essay plan should be a list of brief dot points covering no more than half a page.

- Include your central argument or main contention – a concise statement of your overall response to the topic.
- Write three or four dot points for each paragraph, indicating the main idea and evidence/examples from the text. Note that in your essay you will need to *expand* on these points and *analyse* the evidence.

Structure your essay

An essay is a complete, self-contained piece of writing. It has a clear beginning (the introduction), middle (several body paragraphs) and end (the last paragraph or conclusion). It must also have a central argument that runs throughout, linking each paragraph to form a coherent whole. See examples of introductions and conclusions in the 'Analysing a sample topic' and 'Sample answer' sections.

The introduction establishes your overall response to the topic. It includes your main contention and outlines the main evidence you will refer to in the course of the essay. Write your introduction *after* you have done a plan and *before* you write the rest of the essay.

The body paragraphs argue your case – they present evidence from the text and explain how this evidence supports your argument. Each body paragraph needs:

- a strong **topic sentence** (usually the first sentence) that states the main point being made in the paragraph
- **evidence** from the text, including some brief quotations
- **analysis** of the textual evidence, with **explanation** of its significance and how it supports your argument
- **links back to the topic** in one or more statements, usually towards the end of the paragraph.

Connect the body paragraphs so that your discussion flows smoothly. Use some linking words and phrases such as 'similarly' and 'on the other hand', though don't start every paragraph like this. Another strategy is to use a significant word from the last sentence of one paragraph in the first sentence of the next.

Use key terms from the topic – or synonyms for them – throughout, so the relevance of your discussion to the topic is always clear.

The conclusion ties everything together and finishes the essay. It includes strong statements that emphasise your central argument and provide a clear response to the topic.

Avoid simply restating the points made earlier in the essay – this will end on a very flat note and imply that you have run out of ideas and vocabulary. The conclusion should be a logical extension of what you have written, not just a repetition or summary of it. Writing an effective conclusion can be a challenge. Try using these tips:

- Start by linking back to the final sentence of the second-last paragraph, rather than leaping to your main contention straight away – this helps your writing to flow.
- Use synonyms and expressions with equivalent meanings to vary your vocabulary. This allows you to reinforce your line of argument without being repetitive.
- When planning your essay, think of one or two broad statements or observations about the text's wider meaning. These should be related to the topic and your overall argument. Keep them for the conclusion, since they will give you something 'new' to say but still follow logically from your discussion. The introduction will be focused on the topic, but the conclusion can present a wider view of the text.

Essay topics

1. How is the issue of racism explored through the disappearance of Jedda Gondiwindi?
2. What does *The Yield* say about the impact of colonial gatekeeping on Aboriginal communities?
3. Albert Gondiwindi defines 'yield' as both "the things that man can take from the land" and "the things you give to, the movement, the space between things".
   How are these two definitions explored in the novel?
4. "At the answering of the phone and the breaking of the news, she felt something dark and three-dimensional fall out of her body, something as solid as a self. She'd become *less* suddenly."
   How does *The Yield* explore multiple forms of grief?
5. "The river bends time, what happened at the river goes on for us forever."
   How does time operate in *The Yield*?
6. What role does extinction play in *The Yield*?
7. "[It] was the food that they lived for, the food that they shared with every person who stayed or worked in and around the house – food was the centre."
   What role does food play in *The Yield*?
8. "Once, the ghosts came when I was meant to be doing chores, and away we went to shake a leg."
   What is the significance of the novel's non-realist elements to the narrative?
9. How do the three parts of *The Yield* (August's story, Albert's dictionary and Rev. Greenleaf's letter) tell a bigger story than any one part alone?
10. "For all its sorrow, this is a big hearted, hopeful book. More hopeful, maybe, than we deserve." (Miles Allinson)
    Discuss.

Vocabulary for writing on *The Yield*

Artefacts: The key characteristic of an artefact is that it is formed by humans for human use. As such, artefacts are central to archaeological understandings of civilisations – understandings that can, as *The Yield* indicates, be vital to Native Title claims. The control and display of artefacts in museums is also a subject of some debate, and there are strong calls for artefacts held in museums to be repatriated to the communities from which they were originally taken.

Country: Although this is a term used for geographical spaces relating to Aboriginal groups, 'Country' is not synonymous with 'nation', either linguistically or ideologically. Jeanine Leane writes in 'Tracking Our Country' that 'the continuing settler quest is to "write a nation" because you do have to write nation. In contrast, you do not have to write Country because Country *is* ... In Australia, the nation attempts to write over many Countries' (Leane 2014).

Mission: A mission is an organised effort to promulgate the Christian faith. Missionaries are based at a mission station, sometimes simply called a mission. In *The Yield*, Rev. Greenleaf uses the term 'mission' in both ways: to describe the physical location, Prosperous Mission; and to describe his attempts to bring Christianity to the local Aboriginal people.

Native Title: This varies from country to country, but, broadly speaking, Native Title in Australia is recognition of pre-existing Aboriginal and Torres Strait Islander rights and interests in the land according to traditional laws and customs. Although the foundational case in advancing Native Title rights was *Mabo v Queensland (No. 2)* in 1992, there were several precedents, including a case brought (ultimately unsuccessfully) by Wiradjuri man Paul Coe in the late 1970s.

Stolen Generations: The Aboriginal and Torres Strait Islander children removed from their families between the late 1800s and the 1970s.

Analysing a sample topic

This section leads you through the analysis of a single topic and the planning of a response.

"For all its sorrow, this is a big hearted, hopeful book. More hopeful, maybe, than we deserve." (Miles Allinson)
Discuss.

There are four clear areas to address in this question. Firstly, think about what sorrow means in *The Yield*, and establish the ways in which this is a sorrowful narrative. Secondly, address the question of hope. The following sample approach agrees that *The Yield* is a hopeful book, but this might not be the conclusion of all readers. Thirdly, think about what the term 'we' means, and whether all readers can be combined under this term. If not, how might their experiences and responses differ? Finally, outline a response to the question of whether hope needs to be 'deserved'.

Sample introduction

> *The Yield* deals with traumatic events for the Gondiwindi family, for the Aboriginal people of Massacre Plains more generally and for the town as a whole. Disappearances, deaths, forcible separations and a long drought have all left their mark. Despite this, the novel offers hope in the form of family reunions, the revelation of secrets, reconciliation with the past and the rejuvenation of languages, cultures and communities. But not all readers will perceive the novel's hopefulness in the same way; for some, it may be less clear-cut than for others.

Body paragraph outline

Body paragraph 1: *The Yield* deals with sorrowful subject matter.

- Explain some of the sorrowful subject matter. It may help to think about this in a number of stages.
- Events in the past include the events on the Mission: massacres, assaults, the removal of artefacts and the banning of language.
- Events in the recent past include Jedda's disappearance and Jimmy's death.
- Events in the present include Albert's death and Elsie's grief, August's ongoing struggles, the threat posed by the mine and the loss of Prosperous House.

Body paragraph 2: Despite this sorrow, the novel is hopeful.

- Discuss some of the novel's hopeful aspects. These include, for instance, August's reconciliation with her family, including her mother and her cousin; the truth about Jedda's disappearance being revealed to the family; and August coming to terms with her eating disorder and beginning to overcome it.
- Explain why these are hopeful events. When the family learns the truth about Jedda they find out for certain that she is dead, so why is there an element of hope here (if you believe there is)?

Body paragraph 3: When Allinson says 'we', who does he mean?

- 'We' is a potentially large and diverse readership. Wiradjuri readers will be a different 'we', in this context, from white Australian readers.
- Think about whether the text can be said to appeal to all readers in the same way.

Body paragraph 4: Is this hope something that 'we' deserve?

- Discuss some of the ways in which the novel indicates that gatekeeping and racism are still aspects of life for Aboriginal Australians – this might make some readers question how hopeful the novel really is. Include examples, such as the security guard at the museum and the man in the fish and chip shop.

→

- It is also worth thinking about what hope does: is a hopeful ending something that we 'deserve' (e.g. a reward for good behaviour), or is a hopeful ending a way of inducing good behaviour? That is, are people likely to be more open to change, reconciliation and awareness of past traumas if they are offered hope as an outcome?

Sample conclusion

> It is difficult to say whether we deserve the hopefulness of *The Yield*, given that the book will mean different things to different readers. For some, the prospect of rejuvenated languages and cultures will be important and satisfying, something that may well be earned and help to address trauma, as it does for August Gondiwindi and her family. For others, even if hope is not earned, it may act as a positive spur to action, helping readers to embrace reconciliation and change. Perhaps the hopefulness in *The Yield* is less about what we deserve and more about what we need.

SAMPLE ANSWER

What role does extinction play in *The Yield*?

The concept of extinction is raised a number of times in *The Yield*, in reference to animals, plants, people, culture and language. The concept of extinction allows Winch to explore the devastating and large-scale consequences of colonisation, as well as to explore more personal traumas, such as the loss of family members. However, the novel treats extinction not as inevitable but rather as something that can be avoided, albeit not without hard work and dedication.

The concept of extinction is first raised when August hears the news of Albert 'Poppy' Gondiwindi's death and associates it with a recent newspaper article declaring the black rhino extinct. The newspaper headline emphasises that the rhino is 'gone forever', and August reflects that this is also true of her grandfather. The extinction described here is both global and personal: the black rhino is gone, but so is the unique individual that is Poppy Gondiwindi. Although the narrative does not explicitly state this, the rhino's extinction is also connected to colonisation: once able to roam freely across the African landscape, the rhino population has been affected by the expansion of people into its territory, by farming practices and by poachers.

This connection between the extinction of the rhino and the destruction of Aboriginal Australian peoples and cultures is not a mere coincidence. Like the rhino, Aboriginal Australian people have suffered from the devastating impacts of colonisation, as the novel's three intertwined narratives show. Rev. Greenleaf's letter traces the process whereby white colonisers moved into the land that Aboriginal people occupied and farmed for tens of thousands of years, forcing out the original custodians, placing people in missions and children's homes, breaking up families and destroying the connections between people, culture and language. Albert's dictionary and the narrative focused on August illustrate the damaging effects of these practices on successive generations of Aboriginal people.

Aboriginal people are subjected to violence of all kinds, including massacres, poisoning and sexual assault. Greenleaf's letter graphically depicts the brutal violence of the frontier – 'the cruellest acts that man can inflict upon his fellow man', such as the Station owner's whipping of two teenage boys which continued 'until the second lash had worn out', as well as murder and rape. As Missy examines artefacts in the museum, she hears Albert telling her that blankets were infected with smallpox, and flour and waterholes were poisoned. When August thinks of Poppy Gondiwindi as becoming extinct like the rhino, it is not only a metaphor; she is recalling the actual attempted extinction of the people on Massacre Plains.

It is not only people who can become extinct in *The Yield*, but also culture and language. As with people, this extinction is not an accidental or unintended result. Culture and language are deliberately destroyed, as people are forced from their land and placed in missions and homes where they are forbidden to speak their own language (and made to speak English instead) or to practise their own culture. Both culture and language need to be shared to remain alive, and, in the wake of colonisation, both are threatened with extinction. Plants are also vulnerable, as Albert notes that, after years of wheat-growing, only five per cent of the farm consists of native plants.

Despite the novel's unflinching approach to colonial violence, it nevertheless suggests that processes seemingly leading towards extinction can be reversed. Albert's ancestors refer to him as a man back from extinction, once they have taught him all he needs to know about his culture and his people. Albert in turn passes on what he can, as in the 'Heads, Shoulders, Knees and Toes' song in Wiradjuri language, which all his children and grandchildren remember. His work on the dictionary is described by researchers at the end of the novel as bringing the language back from extinction. Even Albert himself is not entirely extinct at the end of the novel: not only is his recorded voice reading the words of his dictionary, keeping him alive in the town, but he speaks to his daughter Missy as the ancestors spoke to him. He is, in fact, just inhabiting a different way of being.

Extinction plays an important role in *The Yield*, from its first mention in the early pages where August makes a connection between her recently deceased grandfather and the extinct black rhino, through to the final pages where the Gondiwindi family learns of Jedda's death. Winch shows that people, plants, language and culture are all vulnerable to violent dispossession and potential extinction. However, she does not treat extinction as inevitable. As Albert's dictionary is threaded through the narratives of Reverend Greenleaf and August, a language slowly comes back to life. The process of coming back from extinction is difficult but, as Albert's dictionary shows, it can be achieved by those who are sufficiently passionate and dedicated.

REFERENCES & READING

Text

Winch, TJ 2021, *The Yield*, Penguin Books, Melbourne.

References and further reading

Allinson, M 2019, '*The Yield* by Tara June Winch', review, Readings, https://www.readings.com.au/reviews/the-yield-by-tara-june-winch

Bamblett, L 2013, *Our Stories Are Our Survival*, Aboriginal Studies Press, Canberra.

Behrendt, L 2016, *Finding Eliza: Power and Colonial Storytelling*, University of Queensland Press, St Lucia.

Bellette, A 2022, 'Blood and Bone: Unsettling the Settler in Aboriginal Gothic', *Griffith Review*, no. 76, pp.255–64, https://www.griffithreview.com/articles/blood-and-bone/

Clayton, I & Barlow, A 1997, *Wiradjuri of the Rivers and Plains*, Heinemann Library, Port Melbourne.

Coe, M 1986, *Windradyne: A Wiradjuri Koorie*, Blackbooks, Sydney.

Curthoys, A 2002, *Freedom Ride: A Freedom Rider Remembers*, Allen and Unwin, Crows Nest.

Gapps, S 2021, *Gudyarra: The First Wiradyuri War of Resistance – The Bathurst War, 1822–1824*, NewSouth Publishing, Sydney.

Giacon, J & Lowe, K 2017, 'Key Factors in the Renewal of Aboriginal Languages in NSW', *Language, Land and Song*, Endangered Languages Publishing, Australia, pp.523–38.

Heiss, A 2019, *The BlackWords Essays*, St Lucia, AustLit. First published in 2015. https://www.austlit.edu.au/blackwordsessays

——(ed.) 2022, *Growing Up Wiradjuri: Stories from the Wiradjuri Nation*, Magabala Books, Broome.

Kossew, S 2019, 'Precarity and Survival in Tara June Winch's *After the Carnage*', *Australian Humanities Review*, no. 64, http://australianhumanitiesreview.org/wp-content/uploads/2019/05/AHR64_12_Kossew.pdf

Leane, J 2014, 'Tracking Our Country in Settler Literature', *Journal of the Association for the Study of Australian Literature*, vol. 14, no. 3, https://openjournals.library.sydney.edu.au/index.php/JASAL/article/view/10039

——2017, 'The Politics of Memory and Contemporary Aboriginal Women's Writing', *Antipodes*, vol. 31, no. 2, pp.242–51.

Pascoe, B 2014, *Dark Emu*, Magabala Books, Broome.

Sharrad, P 2020, 'Indigenous Transnational: Pluses and Perils, and Tara June Winch', *Transnational Literature*, no. 12.

Tan, M 2016, 'Yamandhu Marang? Language Does Not Belong to People, It Belongs to Country', *The Guardian*, 31 August, https://www.theguardian.com/culture/2016/sep/01/yamandhu-marang-language-does-not-belong-to-people-it-belongs-to-country

Taylor, S 2014, 'Our Mother Tongue: Wiradjuri', *Mother Tongue*, Australian Broadcasting Corporation.